AN

F. SCOTT FITZGERALD

COMPANION

BOOK-OF-THE-MONTH CLUB
NEW YORK

An F. Scott Fitzgerald Companion is a publication of Book-of-the-Month Club, 1271 Avenue of the Americas, New York, NY 10020.

Book design by Felicia Telsey

Printed in the United States of America

CONTENTS

APPENDIX

FITZGERALD AT PRINCETON

BY JOHN PEALE BISHOP

J UST HOW OLD Scott Fitzgerald was when I first met him is a
question. He afterwards said that he had lied so often about
his age that he had to bring his old nurse on from Saint Paul
in order himself to know in just what year he had been born. He
was, as nearly as I can make out, seventeen; but even then he was
determined to be a genius, and since one of the most obvious
characteristics of genius was precocity, he must produce from an
early age. He did, but wanted through vanity to make it even earlier.

Long afterwards, I complained to him that I thought he took seventeen as his norm, making everything later a falling off. For a moment
he demurred, then said, "If you make it fifteen, I will agree with you."

He had, like myself, only arrived at Princeton; the Commons
for Freshmen was not yet open; we sat side by side at a large round
table in a corner at the Peacock Inn. It was the first time I had
gone out alone, for in those opening days we stuck very close to
the boys who had come down from school with us. It was by
chance that I sat next to this youth so quick to conversation; we
stayed on when the others had gone. In the leafy street outside the
September twilight faded; the lights came on against the paper
walls, where tiny peacocks strode and trailed their tails among the
gayer foliations. I learned that Fitzgerald had written a play which

had been performed at school. Places were cleared; other students sat down at the tables around us. We talked of books: those I had read, which were not many, those Fitzgerald had read, which were even less, those he said he had read, which were many, many more. It was the age at which we were discovering Meredith and the writers of the *Yellow Book*. Wells had not yet come, but to the youth from Saint Paul it was soon clear that Compton Mackenzie had.

Fitzgerald was pert and fresh and blond, and looked, as someone said, like a jonquil. He scribbled in class, or sat in an apparent dreaming drowse, from which he was startled from time to time by a question which he had only half heard. Though he arrived at what seemed a clever way of stalling until he could at least guess what had been asked him ("It all depends on how you look at it. There is the subjective and the objective point of view."), it did not prevent his being dropped from the class. He had an ailment, which served as excuse for his departure. Like so many precocious literary talents, he had, I believe, a tendency to tuberculosis. When he returned, it was, so far as the registrar of Princeton was concerned, to take his place in another class. I saw as much of him as ever, perhaps more, for his ambitious political career on the campus had been damaged by his absence.

He left Princeton without a degree and without much of an education; but he had with him the material for two novels. The first, *The Romantic Egoist*, not many have seen in its entirety beside myself, a few old school friends who appeared in it, and the unwilling publishers. It was written on Saturday nights and Sunday afternoons at the Officers' Club at Fort Leavenworth, Kansas, where he was stationed during a period of training as Second Lieutenant in the regular Army. Scraps of it were saved, trimmed, and refurbished to appear here and there as patches in *This Side of Paradise*, a book which, when it appeared, was reviewed by one of the author's Princeton friends, T. K. Whipple, as "The Collected Works of F. Scott Fitzgerald." So it was, for the time being, for not a line from any of those poems scribbled in lecture halls, if it chanced to be good, had been wasted.

—1948

FITZGERALD'S FIRST FLAPPER

BY AMAR SHAH

GINEVRA KING, the beautiful daughter of a rich Lake Forest, Illinois, family, had come to St. Paul, Minnesota, during Christmas 1914 as the house guest of her roommate Marie Hersey. During her stay there Marie introduced Ginevra to a young Princeton undergraduate who would fall in love with her. He would court the debutante with dark curly hair and romantic brown eyes through mail and infrequent visits until January of 1917, when her father informed him, "Poor boys shouldn't think of marrying rich girls." The sad young man would visit and document the traumatic event many times in his future literary career.

The spirit of Ginevra King would haunt F. Scott Fitzgerald's fiction. She was the pioneering embodiment of his trademark heroine, and the muse whose melodic song he listed to long before the mythic romance with his beloved Zelda.

Ginevra was the original princess in the king's castle. His golden girl. She was sixteen and a student at the prestigious Westover School in Middlebury, Connecticut, when she met Scott, who was known in his hometown of St. Paul as the man who had made it big at Princeton writing lyrics for the theatrical Triangle Club. Ginevra was the future flapper of his fiction, daring, reckless, rich,

3

beautiful—although not necessarily damned.

Fitzgerald was enamored with the femme fatale, the young girl whose unscrupulousness and seductive allure captivated her prey. Ginevra personified the paragon. With her locked in as his muse, Fitzgerald rose socially in the land of spires and gargoyles. He made the prestigious Cottage Club, was elected as secretary of the Triangle, and chosen for the editorial board of *The Tiger.* He would see Ginevra at football games and dances. He later wrote that he never forgot "one night when she made luminous the Ritz Roof."

However, his ambition would be stifled in November 1916 because of academic failure and illness. "I had lost certain offices, the chief one as the presidency of the Triangle Club," Fitzgerald wrote in his famous *Crack-up* essays. "To me college would never be the same. There were to be no badges of pride, no models, after all . . . I had lost every single thing I wanted." Including Ginevra.

He never recovered from the jolt. He said he had become a different person, and that a new person would find new things to care about. He became the voice of his generation but he'd never forget the girl whose rejection brought him there.

Ginevra was the model for Isabel in Fitzgerald's first novel, *This Side of Paradise.* She would appear as the vindictive Judy Jones in his story "Winter Dreams." He would use her again as the archetype for Josephine Perry, the female counterpart in his Basil Duke Lee stories. And Fitzgerald speaks about his character's attraction for the type of girl Ginevra was in his last college story, "The Pierian Springs and the Last Straw":

> All the time I was idealizing her to the last possibility, I was perfectly conscious that she was about the faultiest girl I'd ever met. She was selfish, conceited, and uncontrolled, and since these were my own faults I was doubly aware of them. Yet I never wanted to change her . . . She had the strongest effect on me. She made me want to do something for her, to get something to show her. Every honor in college took on the semblance of a presentable trophy.

In 1918 he received news from Marie Hersey that Ginevra was getting married. Fitzgerald was invited. He didn't go. In his ledgers he kept the invitation and wedding announcement. That year he also met a young southern belle named Zelda Sayre.

Much later, in 1937, Fitzgerald wrote his daughter Scottie about the possibility of a rendezvous with Ginevra:

> Then I didn't see her for twenty-one years, although I tele-phoned her in 1933 to entertain your mother at the World's Fair, which she did. Yesterday I get a wire that she is in Santa Barbara and will I come down there immediate-ly. She was the first girl I ever loved and I have faithfully avoided seeing her up to this moment to keep the illusion perfect, because she ended up throwing me over with the most supreme boredom and indifference. I don't know whether I should go or not. It would be very, very strange. These great beauties are often something else at thirty-eight, but Ginevra had a great deal besides beauty.

He did go. She was still beautiful.

In their correspondence, Fitzgerald saved every letter Ginevra wrote him. He later had them typed up and bound with ribbon. Not a single one of Scott's letters to her survived. She threw all of them away.

—2000

SCOTT FITZGERALD

FROM
A MOVEABLE FEAST

BY ERNEST HEMINGWAY

In this excerpt from his great memoir of Paris in the 1920s, A Moveable Feast, *Ernest Hemingway writes about an eventful road trip with his new friend F. Scott Fitzgerald.*

ITZGERALD TOLD ME that he and Zelda, his wife, had been compelled to abandon their small Renault motor car in Lyon because of bad weather and he asked me if I would go down to Lyon with him on the train to pick up the car and drive up with him to Paris. The Fitzgeralds had rented a furnished flat at 14 rue de Tilsitt not far from the Etoile. It was late spring now and I thought the country would be at its best and we could have an excellent trip. Scott seemed so nice and so reasonable, and I had watched him drink two good solid whiskies and nothing happened, and his charm and his seeming good sense made the other night at the Dingo seem like an unpleasant dream. So I said I would like to go down to Lyon with him and when did he want to leave.

We agreed to meet the next day and we then arranged to leave for Lyon on the express train that left in the morning. This train left at a convenient hour and was very fast. It made only one stop,

7

as I recall, at Dijon. We planned to get into Lyon, have the car checked and in good shape, have an excellent dinner and get an early-morning start back towards Paris.

I was enthusiastic about the trip. I would have the company of an older and successful writer, and in the time we would have to talk in the car I would certainly learn much that it would be useful to know. It is strange now to remember thinking of Scott as an older writer, but at the time, since I had not yet read *The Great Gatsby,* I thought of him as a much older writer. I thought he wrote *Saturday Evening Post* stories that had been readable three years before but I never thought of him as a serious writer. He had told me at the Closerie des Lilas how he wrote what he thought were good stories, and which really were good stories for the *Post,* and then changed them for submission, knowing exactly how he must make the twists that made them into salable magazine stories. I had been shocked at this and I said I thought it was whoring. He said it was whoring but that he had to do it as he made his money from the magazines to have money ahead to write decent books. I said that I did not believe anyone could write any way except the very best he could write without destroying his talent. Since he wrote the real story first, he said, the destruction and changing of it that he did at the end did him no harm. I could not believe this and I wanted to argue him out of it but I needed a novel to back up my faith and to show him and convince him, and I had not yet written any such novel. . . .

On the morning we were to leave from the Gare de Lyon I arrived in plenty of time and waited outside the train gates for Scott. He was bringing the tickets. When it got close to the time for the train to leave and he had not arrived, I bought an entry ticket to the track and walked along the side of the train looking for him. I did not see him and as the long train was about to pull out I got aboard and walked through the train hoping only that he would be aboard. It was a long train and he was not on it. I explained the situation to the conductor, paid for a ticket, second class—there was no third—and asked the conductor for the name of the best hotel in Lyon. There was nothing to do but wire Scott from Dijon giving him the address of the hotel where I would wait for him in Lyon. He would not get it before he left, but his wife would be presumed to wire it on to him. I had never heard, then, of a grown man missing a train; but on this trip I was to learn many new things.

In those days I had a very bad, quick temper, but by the time we were through Montereau it had quieted down and I was not too angry to watch and enjoy the countryside and at noon I had a good lunch in the dining car and drank a bottle of St.-Émilion and thought that even if I had been a damned fool to accept an invitation for a trip that was to be paid for by someone else, and was spending money on it that we needed to go to Spain, it was a good lesson for me. I had never before accepted an invitation to go on any trip that was paid for, instead of the cost split, and in this one I had insisted that we split the cost of the hotels and meals. But now I did not know whether Fitzgerald would even show up. While I had been angry I had demoted him from Scott to Fitzgerald. Later I was delighted that I had used up the anger at the start and gotten it over with. It was not a trip designed for a man easy to anger.

In Lyon I learned that Scott left Paris for Lyon but had left no word as to where he was staying. I confirmed my address there and the servant said she would let him know if he called. Madame was not well and was still sleeping. I called all the name hotels and left messages but could not locate Scott and then I went out to a café to have an apéritif and read the papers. . . .

There was no word from Scott [back] at the hotel and I went to bed in the unaccustomed luxury of the hotel and read a copy of the first volume of *A Sportsman's Sketches* by Turgenev that I had borrowed from Sylvia Beach's library. I had not been in the luxury of a big hotel for three years and I opened the windows wide and rolled up the pillows under my shoulders and head and was happy being with Turgenev in Russia until I was asleep while still reading. I was shaving in the morning getting ready to go out for breakfast when they called from the desk saying a gentleman was downstairs to see me.

"Ask him to come up, please," I said and went on shaving, listening to the town which had come heavily alive since early morning.

Scott did not come up and I met him down at the desk.

"I'm terribly sorry there was this mix-up," he said. "If I had only known what hotel you were going to it would have been simple."

"That's all right," I said. We were going to have a long ride and I was all for peace. "What train did you come down on?"

"One not long after the one you took. It was a very comfortable train and we might just as well have come down together."

"Have you had breakfast?"

"Not yet. I've been hunting all over the town for you."

"That's a shame," I said. "Didn't they tell you at home that I was here?"

"No. Zelda wasn't feeling well and I probably shouldn't have come. The whole trip has been disastrous so far."

"Let's get some breakfast and find the car and roll," I said.

"That's fine. Should we have breakfast here?"

"It would be quicker in a café."

"But we're sure to get a good breakfast here."

"All right."

It was a big American breakfast with ham and eggs and it was very good. But by the time we had ordered it, waited for it, eaten it, and waited to pay for it, close to an hour had been lost. It was not until the waiter came with the bill that Scott decided that we have the hotel make us a picnic lunch. I tried to argue him out of this as I was sure we could get a bottle of Mâcon in Mâcon and we could buy something to make sandwiches in a *charcuterie*. Or, if things were closed when we went through, there would be any number of restaurants where we could stop on our way. But he said I had told him that the chicken was wonderful in Lyon and that we should certainly take one with us. So the hotel made us a lunch that could not have cost us very much more than four or five times what it would have cost us if we had bought it ourselves.

Scott had obviously been drinking before I met him and, as he looked as though he needed a drink, I asked him if he did not want one in the bar before we set out. He told me he was not a morning drinker and asked if I was. I told him it depended entirely on how I felt and what I had to do and he said that if I felt that I needed a drink, he would keep me company so I would not have to drink alone. So we had a whisky and Perrier in the bar while we waited for the lunch and both felt much better.

I paid for the hotel room and the bar, although Scott wanted to pay for everything. Since the start of the trip I had felt a little complicated about it emotionally and I found I felt much better the more things I could pay for. I was using up the money we had saved for Spain, but I knew I had good credit with Sylvia Beach and could borrow and repay whatever I was wasting now.

At the garage where Scottie had left the car, I was astonished to find that the small Renault had no top. The top had been damaged in unloading the car in Marseilles, or it had been damaged in Marseilles in some manner and Zelda had ordered it cut away and refused to have it replaced. His wife hated car tops, Scott told me, and without the top they had driven as far as Lyon where they were halted by the rain. The car was in fair shape otherwise and Scott paid the bill after disputing several charges for washing, greasing, and for adding two liters of oil. The garage man explained to me that the car needed new piston rings and had evidently been run without sufficient oil and water. He showed me how it had heated up and burned the paint off the motor. He said if I could persuade Monsieur to have a ring job done in Paris, the car, which was a good little car, would be able to give the service it was built for.

"Monsieur would not let me replace the top."

"No?"

"One has an obligation to a vehicle."

"One has."

"You gentlemen have no waterproofs?"

"No," I said. "I did not know about the top."

"Try and make Monsieur be serious," he said pleadingly. "At least about the vehicle."

"Ah," I said.

We were halted by rain about an hour north of Lyon.

In that day we were halted by rain possibly ten times. They were passing showers and some of them were longer than others. If we had waterproof coats it would have been pleasant enough to drive in that spring rain. As it was we sought the shelter of trees or halted at cafés alongside the road. We had a marvelous lunch from the hotel at Lyon, an excellent truffled roast chicken, delicious bread and white Mâcon wine and Scott was very happy when we drank the white Mâconnais at each of our stops. At Mâcon I had bought four more bottles of excellent wine which I uncorked as we needed them.

I am not sure Scott had ever drunk wine from a bottle before and it was exciting to him as though he were slumming or as a girl might be excited by going swimming for the first time without a bathing suit. But, by early afternoon, he had begun to worry about his health. He told me about two people who had died of congestion of the lungs recently. Both of them had died in Italy and he had been deeply impressed.

I told him that congestion of the lungs was an old-fashioned term for pneumonia, and he told me that I knew nothing about it and was absolutely wrong. Congestion of the lungs was a malady which was indigenous to Europe and I could not possibly know anything about it even if I had read my father's medical books, since they dealt with diseases that were strictly American. I said that my father had studied in Europe too. But Scott explained that congestion of the lungs had only appeared in Europe recently and that my father could not possibly have known anything about it. He also explained that diseases were different in different parts of America, and if my father had practiced medicine in New York instead of in the Middle West, he would have known an entirely different gamut of diseases. He used the word gamut.

I said that he had a good point in the prevalence of certain diseases in one part of the United States and their absence in others and cited the amount of leprosy in New Orleans and its low incidence, then, in Chicago. But I said that doctors had a system of exchange of knowledge and information among themselves and now that I remembered it after he had brought it up, I had read the authoritative article on congestion of the lungs in Europe in the *Journal of the American Medical Association* which traced its history back to Hippocrates himself. This held him for a while and I urged him to take another drink of Mâcon, since a good white wine, moderately full-bodied but with a low alcoholic content, was almost a specific against the disease.

Scott cheered a little after this but he began to fail again shortly and asked me if we would make a big town before the onset of the fever and delirium by which, I had told him, the true congestion of the lungs, European, announced itself. I was now translating from an article which I had read in a French medical journal on the same malady while waiting at the American Hospital in Neuilly to have my throat cauterized, I told him. A word like cauterized had a comforting effect on Scott. But he wanted to know when we would make the town. I said if we pushed on we should make it in twenty-five minutes to an hour.

Scott then asked me if I were afraid to die and I said more at some times than at others.

It now began to rain really heavily and we took refuge in the next village at a café. I cannot remember all the details of that afternoon but when we were finally in a hotel at what must have been Châlon-sur-Saône, it was so late that the drug stores were closed. Scott had undressed and gone to bed as soon as we reached the hotel. He did not mind dying of congestion of the lungs, he said. It was only the question of who was to look after Zelda and young Scottie. I did not see very well how I could look after them since I was having a healthily rough time looking after my wife Hadley and young son Bumby, but I said I would do my best and Scott thanked me. I must see that Zelda did not drink and that Scottie should have an English governess.

We had sent our clothes to be dried and were in our pajamas. It was still raining outside but it was cheerful in the room with the electric light on. Scott was lying in bed to conserve his strength for his battle against the disease. I had taken his pulse, which was seventy-two, and had felt his forehead, which was cool. I had listened to his chest and had him breathe deeply, and his chest sounded all right.

"Look, Scott," I said. "You're perfectly O.K. If you want to do the best thing to keep from catching cold, just stay in bed and I'll order us each a lemonade and a whisky and you take an aspirin with yours and you'll feel fine and won't even get a cold in your head."

"Those old wives' remedies," Scott said.

"You haven't any temperature. How the hell are you going to have congestion of the lungs without a temperature?"

"Don't swear at me," Scott said. "How do you know I haven't a temperature?"

"Your pulse is normal and you haven't any fever to the touch."

"To the touch," Scott said bitterly. "If you're a real friend, get me a thermometer."

"I'm in pajamas."

"Send for one."

I rang for the waiter. He didn't come and I rang again and then went down the hallway to look for him. Scott was lying with his eyes closed, breathing slowly and carefully and, with his waxy color and his perfect features, he looked like a little dead crusader. I was getting tired of the literary life, if this was the literary life that I was leading, and already I missed not working and I felt the death loneliness that comes at the end of every day that is wasted in your life.

F. SCOTT FITZGERALD
THE MAN AND HIS WORK

BY ALFRED KAZIN

This piece originally appeared as the introduction to F. Scott Fitzgerald: The Man and His Work, *a 1951 book edited by Kazin that contained a collection of critical pieces about Fitzgerald.*

". . . the stamp that goes into my books so that people can read it blind like Braille."

—Fitzgerald: Notebooks

WHEN YOU GO BACK now to the old records and reviews from the twenties—back to the yellowing newspaper gossip about Scott and Zelda jumping out of sheer exuberance into the fountain outside the Plaza; the condescending literary columns that once glittered with all the paste jewels of the period but are now as dim as the stone plaque in Cartier's commemorating the visit of Queen Marie of Roumania; the deathless views of *The Independent* in 1925 that *The Great Gatsby* is another of Fitzgerald's "sophisticated juveniles" or Mrs. Isabel Paterson's historic pronouncement that "it is a book of the season only"—your first thought, actually, is how alive to his quality as a writer, how generous to his every achievement, Fitzgerald's critics were then.

Of course they thought him a great big kid and recklessly wasteful of his talent. And inevitably, his personal legend interested them as much as his books did. With his uncannily representative good looks—"Scott really looks . . . as the undergraduate would like to look," John C. Mosher noted about him in *The New Yorker*—his equally vivid wife, his instant success as "the voice of the postwar generation," his violent delight in the "gorgeous" twenties, he could no more help arousing attention and endless gossip than did the Jay Gatsby in whose brain "a universe of ineffable gaudiness spun itself out. . . ." Everything about him was on our most picturesque national scale; it was as if the growing self-confidence of American writers and the unashamed veneration of wealth had suddenly met in this son of genteel poverty from St. Paul. In those days Fitzgerald seemed to have come out of the Middle West, Princeton, the prom halls and football stadiums wrapped in all the rich colors of American wealth from McKinley to Harding, hungry for every privilege and daring every disaster, ready to satisfy the usual American craving for a novelist who would be one "of our own," thoroughly *in* the national life, and responsive to all its popular idols.

The critics like to josh him. "I'm the only one [of the younger generation] that's discouraged," Edmund Wilson has him say in the imaginary dialogue with Van Wyck Brooks, "because I find that I can't live down at Great Neck on anything under thirty-six thousand a year and I have to write a lot of rotten stuff that bores me and makes me depressed." He was so much the professionally successful American author trying to beat the old masters, was so poisonously bright and yet so fluently and vulnerably self-absorbed, that he flattered every writer of his own generation into feeling old and wise. Sometimes, like his college friend Wilson, whom in his bitterest despair he was to salute as his "intellectual conscience," the critics seemed to know him as a man altogether so well that they could not help sounding surprised by every fresh example of his talent—a natural fault in critics faced with a writer who seems to have *nothing* but talent. But these good critics were too full of their own work, and too happy in the promise of the period, to grudge him anything.

They were naturally generous and enthusiastic in a way serious critics of fiction are not today, for they felt themselves part of an exciting new movement in the American novel. It was even a joke on the copybook traditions of the past that Scott Fitzgerald should be so good; he spelled badly, he read little, his faking and his snobbery were awful. But he was American youth writing—with a freshness of feeling and a miraculously intact belief in romantic love that made the critics see through the college-lit. exhibitionism in *This Side of Paradise*. They recognized that Fitzgerald was better than he allowed himself to be. He was the shining boy, already the Chatterton of our literature, who even at college had known that he wanted to be "one of the greatest writers who have ever lived." His very disharmonies were national, made Americans feel closer to him than they usually do to a writer; he thought literature could buy him a place like any movie star's or debutante's in the high world of American fashion. You sense the protectiveness in so warm a tribute to him before *Gatsby* as Paul Rosenfeld's, and in the kindly *New Yorker* profile by John C. Mosher, written around the then unbelievable fact that Scott Fitzgerald was almost thirty. The critics were eager to note every improvement in style, every sign of developing maturity, from *This Side of Paradise* to *The Beautiful and Damned*, a book it is impossible to read now without feeling very remote from the early Fitzgerald—or is it only from 1922?

There was often regret, and continuing exasperation, that he spent so much of himself writing for the slicks. But by 1925, with *The Great Gatsby*, he had earned the full respect of those "writing friends" who, as Glenway Wescott was to say at the time of his death, "thought he had the best narrative gift of the century." These "writing friends" were his nearest critics, his most loyal, and in many respects his best—the analogy to Marlowe with which

John Dos Passos concludes his tribute to Fitzgerald here is one of the most hauntingly right things ever said about him. And how rich Fitzgerald was in those friends—from Wilson and John Peale Bishop at college to Gertrude Stein, Hemingway, Lardner, Dos Passos, and others; how clearly he was their "darling," their "genius," just as he was only too soon to become their "fool." When, in 1940, the smugly contemptuous reviews so infuriated his friends, and Westbrook Pegler explained him as one "of a queer bunch of undisciplined brats" who had needed "a kick in the pants and a clout over the scalp," it was stirring to see what a company could rally to his defense in *The New Republic.*. The curious coldness in those tributes toward Fitzgerald himself is something else again. The point here is that in the twenties those who really did most for good writing—like Gertrude Stein; who were most conscientious in applying living standards, like Edmund Wilson; to say nothing of Hemingway, who directly learned from him—knew how good he was, encouraged him, and could assist him.

It was once said by the late Peter Monro Jack, who thought Fitzgerald might have been the Proust of his generation, that his misfortunes were due to a lack of constructive and helpful criticism. Of course no writer ever gets enough of this—perhaps not even a Maupassant working directly under Flaubert, or an Eliot revising and cutting *The Waste Land* under the tutelage of Ezra Pound. And certainly much of the criticism written about Fitzgerald during the twenties was admiring but frivolous; probably no other writer, except Whitman, has been made the occasion for so many banalities on the tendency of life in the United States. Yet it was in the very nature of Fitzgerald's work, and of his delirious early success, that the relationship of his critics to him should be more intimate than profound, and after his death, alien to him even when it was deeply reflective. Besides, pleasing as it is to the vanity of critics to think that writers can learn from them, many novelists are impervious to criticism, and some should be. (If William Faulkner had taken seriously half the things written about him in this country between 1925 and 1945, he would never have moved an inch.) There are no general laws in these matters, any more than there are "lessons of craft" for a serious novelist today in all the long overdue praise that is now being rendered up to the shade of Henry James. Everything depends on the specific needs and intelligence of the writer himself. It was usually Fitzgerald who taught his more durable contemporaries. His ability to learn for himself, and to discipline himself, was amazing. In less than five years, despite his pranks and his continual waste of himself, he moved from the juvenility in *This Side of Paradise* to the compressed, deeply moving poet's economy of *The Great Gatsby*. Even when he was sick and desperate, he worked his way through the open anxieties of *Tender Is the Night* to the biting authenticity of *The Last Tycoon*, some of whose pages have the eerie clarity of a man writing from hell.

I wonder what Fitzgerald would have done with more "constructive" criticism. For surely it was not the lack of artistic insight that ailed him, but his spiritual condition; not "discipline" as such (which no writer can arbitrarily impose on his work) that he needed, but some inner purification and resoluteness, the courage "to put the old white light on the home of my heart." He knew what the trouble was; writers always do, though a writer like Fitzgerald is usually less capable of doing anything about it than others are, for he digs dangerously into himself for every story, and writing becomes a constant drain on his emotional capital. One of the most naturally sentient novelists we have ever had, he had to think like a salesman—what Mark Schorer here calls his "snide charlatanism"—to show that he was on to every smart perception that was a condition for survival in the world he loved. He said it all in a letter to his daughter written a few months before his death: ". . . I wish now I'd *never* relaxed or looked back—but said at the end of *The Great Gatsby*: 'I've found my line—from now on this comes first. This is my immediate duty—without this I'm nothing.' " To be a Proust you have, at the very least, to give up the world and give in to the "tyrant" of your intelligence, even if it threatens to devour you. Far from giving up his world—and where would he have been without it? he was about as metaphysical in his tastes as Franklin D. Roosevelt—he could never make up his mind (until it was made up for him, by the nearness of death) whether he was Jay Gatsby trying to win back the love of his life from the rich, or Dick Diver bestowing his "trick of the heart" on the shallow fashionables along the Riviera, or Monroe Stahr trying to do an honest inside job in Hollywood. And it is to be noticed that richer and subtler as the novels become, the heroes grow progressively more alone, because more aware—Fitzgerald's synonym for a state near to death.

That fear of awareness and aloneness is in our culture; Fitzgerald's critics could not have helped him there. For as they emphasize here over and again, he wanted two different things equally well—and though his art found its "tensile balance" in this conflict, it certainly exhausted him as a man. There was a headlong fatality about him which, in the long silence between *The Great Gatsby* and *Tender Is the Night*, the critics could only watch in amazement, some in derision.

It was then, in the thirties, when he cracked like a "plate" and *Tender Is the Night* was generally reviewed as if the critics were trying to blame on Fitzgerald the sins they wished they had committed in the twenties, that he could have used some constructive and helpful criticism. And even this he could still get from a "writing friend" like Hemingway, who told him, very rightly, that "you are twice as good now as at the time you think you were so marvellous." But by his fatal ability to synchronize his most private fortunes and misfortunes with the pattern of each decade he wrote in, Fitzgerald's collapse served the critics of the thirties only too well. It was a time when many who sat in judgment over him showed that they actually feared fresh individual writing. Only a few reviewers, notably John Chamberlain and C. Hartley Grattan, publicly recognized the emotional depth and active social intelligence of *Tender Is the Night* as well as its more obvious neuroticism. Some of the things written about Fitzgerald in the thirties—especially the never-to-be-forgotten "interview" with him featured on the front page of the *New York Evening Post*, September 25, 1936, which portrayed him as a hopeless drunk crying he would never write again—were in the tone usually reserved by tabloid sports reporters for broken-down fighters. Still, it must be admitted that if it was the fashion then to say that he was finished as a creative writer, Fitzgerald himself often seemed to be leading the chorus.

After his death in 1940—specifically, with the publication of *The Last Tycoon* in 1941 and, in 1945, the personal documents Edmund Wilson assembled in *The Crack-up* along with the title essay—critics began again to do him justice on a wide scale. But as late as 1944, Charles Weir, Jr., had still to say that "interest in Fitzgerald dies hard." And it has been noticed that some of the first tributes, originally published in reply to the newspaper articles—"LOST GENERATION LOSES ITS PROPHET," ran the head on one obituary, "NOVELIST VICTIM OF DESPAIR HE DEPICTED"—tend to brood brilliantly over Fitzgerald's tragedy without betraying any great affection for him; John O'Hara opened up with "It is granted that Scott Fitzgerald was not a lovable man." I am sure he was not. But you cannot in one decade think of a writer as the height of American good fortune, and in another see him with fluent self-pity accepting his scapegoat role, without at last, simply enough, wearying of the man who has filled out so many stereotypes for you.

There is ill-concealed exasperation even in some of the more affirmative essays written after *The Last Tycoon* and *The Crack-up*. One reason for this is Fitzgerald's "romanticism." This term has always been meaningless when applied to our literary history, but it has a special sting now both in our hardboiled culture (*Time*, for example, once disposed of Fitzgerald as "the last U.S. Romantic") and in our academic literary culture, where it conveys a distrust of personal expressiveness. Another reason for the continuing impatience with Fitzgerald is that there is not always as much to say about his work as critics would like. Serious criticism of fiction in America today has no sense of assisting a creative movement; it footnotes the old masters. It insists on explanations of the creative achievement in fiction even when there may be none easily forthcoming, and tends to distrust, just a little, a writer who constantly crossed and recrossed the border line between highbrow and popular literature in this country, and who actually wrote some of his best stories for the smooth-paper magazines. But Fitzgerald is one of those novelists whom it is easier to appreciate than to explain, and whom it is possible, and even fascinating, to read over and over—it has often been remarked that *Tender Is the Night* grows better on each re-reading—without always being able to account for the sources of your pleasure.

At first glance there may seem to be a certain duplication in these late essays [in the book *F. Scott Fitzgerald: The Man and His Work*], for many of them were written around *The Crack-up* and necessarily go over the same ground, though certainly not from the same point of view. Fitzgerald did not leave a great body of work; his range was narrow and the highlights are obvious. There are not many hidden details in his work to uncover—though critics *will* try to find more in, say, his Catholicism than he ever put into it— or subtle connections between the books to be traced, as is the case with Faulkner. And unlike Faulkner, Wolfe, Steinbeck, Hemingway, and even Dashiell Hammett, Fitzgerald has never interested many Europeans.[1] So these last essays are largely a commemorative offering to Fitzgerald, across the generations, by

---

[1] Probably because his work enters into specifically American veins of feeling, and is not symbolic enough "about" America—one of its incidental virtues. Moreover, he is too elegant a writer to satisfy the usual European demand that an American writer be broad as the prairies, and too shallow, as compared with Faulkner, to satisfy the new European demand, in the age of Hitler and Stalin, that he reveal those primitive faculties that have burst through the thin crust of nineteenth-century humanism. In these matters one must always remember that if André Gide prefers reading Dashiell Hammett to eulogizing Henry James, it is because Hammett gives him the shock he expects from all things

American critics who are anywhere from ten to twenty-five years younger than he, who generally admire his sensibility, and who feel that now, with all the late returns in, they can address themselves to the deepest sources of his life. And in this, quite apart from their host of independent insights, lies the fascination of these essays, even of their seeming duplication. For they return again and again to the fact that in a land of promise, "failure" will always be a classic theme. And that the modern American artist's struggle for integrity against the foes in his own household shows its richest meaning in a writer like Fitzgerald, who found those foes in his own heart. These late essays round out an historical cycle—not simply from war to war, or from success to neglect to revival, as it is now the fashion to do, we are so hungry for real writers—but from American to American, from self to self.

—1951

American, James's practice of the novel is nothing Gide did not venerate before. There seemed to me no reason for reprinting more than usually trite generalizations about Fitzgerald and the jazz age simply because they had been written first in exquisite French.

The English, who approach everything American these days with distrust, but at least try to read our writers on their merits, have recently come to see how much Fitzgerald is in their particular tradition. His main literary food was the English romantic poets and the twentieth-century English novelists who were particularly influential here just before the First World War—Conrad, Wells, Compton Mackenzie.

THAT SAD YOUNG MAN

BY JOHN CHAPIN MOSHER

ALL WAS QUIET ON the Riviera, and then the Fitzgeralds arrived, Scott and Zelda and Scottie. The summer season opened. There had been talk about their coming. They were coming; they were not. One day they appeared on the beach. They had played tennis the day before, and were badly burned. Everybody was concerned about their burns. They must keep their shoulders covered; they must rub on olive oil. Scott was too burned to go in the water, and much of the time, he sat aside from the rush of things, a reflective, staid paterfamilias.

That the Fitzgeralds are the best-looking couple in modern literary society doesn't do them justice, knowing what we do about beauty and brains. That they might be the handsomest pair at any collegiate houseparty, inspiring alumni to warnings about the pitfalls ahead of the young, is more to the point, although Scott really looks more as the undergraduate would like to look, than the way he generally does. It takes some years of training as the best host of the younger set, and as a much photographed and paragraphed author, to be quite so affable and perfectly at ease with all the world.

Scott feels that he is getting on in years, that he is no longer

25

young. It weighs upon him, troubles him. He is almost thirty. Seldom has he allowed a person of such advanced age to enter his books.

"I have written a story. It is not about the younger generation. The hero is twenty-nine."

It must be some comfort to him that he is so superbly preserved, so stocky, muscular, clear-skinned, with wide, fresh, green-blue eyes, hair blond not grey, with no lines of worry or senility, no saggings anywhere. Mrs. Fitzgerald doesn't show her age either; she might be in her teens. Perhaps Scottie does. Yes, there is no denying she looks her four.

There were rumors that Scott had had a sip or two of something up in Paris and had come South to rest. No one could have guessed it, but he is summary with any such doubts:

"Don't you know I am one of the most notorious drinkers of the younger generation?"

There have been whispers certainly. But the young man who drives his publicity manager into a lake, as Scott once did, is bound to get some reputation of that sort. There was no reason on this occasion why he should not have turned the car to the right as most people did, and as the publicity man comfortably expected, but having had perhaps a cocktail or two, it seemed more amusing to turn to the left off the road. The publicity man was not drowned however.

That was after one of those Long Island parties which established his place before the world as a host. If he is worried now about the advancing years he had better buy up two or three Biltmores before he extends that general invitation:

"Grow old along with me!
The best is yet to be—"

This popularity on two continents may explain something of the financial mystery which so appalls him. Ever since *This Side of Paradise*, money has poured in upon this young couple, thousands and thousands a month. And just as fast it has poured out. Where it goes, no one seems to know. Least of all, evidently, the Fitzgeralds. They complain that nothing is left to show for it. Mrs. Fitzgerald hasn't even a pearl necklace.

According to Scott he has known poverty. There was the terrible winter after the war, when he wanted to marry Zelda, and had only a ninety-dollar-a-month advertising job and no prospects. He had gone South to see her, and when they parted at the station he hadn't even enough money for a Pullman. He had to climb into a Pullman, and then sneak through into the day coach.

It was then that he saw that advertising did not pay, and he threw up that job and went home to St. Paul to write a novel. Statistics show that 12,536 young men annually throw up their jobs and go back home to write a novel. This has all come about since Fitzgerald set the example, for the book he wrote that winter was *This Side of Paradise*, and he was launched.

His success as an author was a great surprise to the home circle. He had always lived in St. Paul, but the Fitzgeralds were not what is known as literary people, in spite of their descent from the author of the "Star Spangled Banner." Scott's father was in business, and Scott was never addicted to prowling about the public library. He was much too attractive a boy to be allowed much seclusion.

However he did enjoy scrawling notebooks full of various suggestions and impressions and witticisms, when the other faithful students of the St. Paul Academy and later those of the Newman School as well were busy adding and subtracting and wondering over what takes the ablative. In the Newman School he decided to run off a musical comedy, and two years later he spent his whole Freshman year at Princeton writing the Triangle Show, which left him no time for algebra, trigonometry, co-ordinate geometry and hygiene. But the Triangle Club accepted the show, and he tutored his way back to college and acted in his own work as a chorus girl.

The war came next, and as Aide-de-Camp to General J. F. Ryan he was able to spend his Saturday afternoons writing a hundred and twenty-thousand word novel, *The Romantic Egoist*, which was merely a preparatory exercise apparently. Publishers thought it original and very well written but not quite what they were looking for at the moment. A great many publishers were in that frame of mind about it, but they did not manage to extinguish the writing impetus in him. The winter after the war, before he took up advertising, he collected 122 rejection slips, and by way of encouragement sold one story for $30.

Never has he lived that amorphous affair known as the literary life. He is too active for that, and too gregarious. To the younger set of St. Paul he was known as a dining-out, dancing-out country-club boy, and it was a surprise when it was said about that he wanted to write. But literary people there didn't take his ambitions as a joke. He became a great friend of Charles Flandrau's, who twenty years ago published *Harvard Episodes*, stories of freshmen and sophomores, done somewhat in the Henry James manner. There is no resemblance between the Flandrau book and Fitzgerald's, but with Mr. Flandrau, Scott found a sympathetic and intelligent critic, someone who could understand why he chose rather to write than to sell bonds. He had already begun to work with an energy unflagging in spite of his invitations to dinner. It sustained him even through the arduous business of rewriting *This Side of Paradise*, changing it, at his publisher's advice, from the first to the third person.

Such application, of course, is not associated with the temperament of any merely clever young man. The popular picture of a blond boy scribbling off best sellers in odd moments between parties is nonsense. He's a very grave, hardworking man, and shows it. In fact there is definitely the touch of the melancholy often obvious upon him.

He is wary of the limitations of his experience.

Very deliberately he has taken as the field for his talent the great story of American wealth. His research is in the chronicles of the big business juntos of the last fifty years; and the drama of high finance, with the personalities of the major actors, Harriman, Morgan, Hill, is his serious study. He saw how the money was being spent; he has made it his business to ferret out how it was cornered.

Although Mrs. Fitzgerald once bought a bond, no young people, with such an income, are more far removed from the ordinary affairs of business. A twenty-dollar-a-week clerk must know more of the practical business world than Scott Fitzgerald who cannot live on thirty thousand a year, and yet who earns every cent he has.

His information, to be sure, on the general history of this American phase is remarkable. His most trivial stories have a substantial substratum of information.

It should yield more and more revealing, penetrating pictures of American life as he settles gravely down in the twilight of the thirties.

—1926

FITZGERALD IN HOLLYWOOD

BY BUDD SCHULBERG

W HEN I WAS LEAVING for New York a few months ago I
said goodbye to Scott and asked him how his novel
was coming. It was the end of the day and he looked
weary, for the writing didn't come so easy anymore. It was a page
a day now, but a *good* page, no matter what the fortunately anony-
mous *Times* and *Tribune* reporters and the unfortunately bylined
Westbrook Pegler [a controversial syndicated columnist of the time]
think. "Oh, slowly," said Scott. "But I'm having a good time with
it. The first draft will be finished by the time you get back. You can
read it then, if you'd like."

That was late in November [1940]. Three weeks later I was
having a drink at Hanover, New Hampshire, with a Dartmouth
professor who suddenly but terribly casually looked up from his
glass and said, "Isn't it too bad about Scott Fitzgerald?" And I
thought of the time, exactly two years before, when Scott was talking to me in that same town, up in the attic of the Hanover Inn.
We (I shudder even now at the incongruity) were collaborating on
a moving picture of college life which we had been imported from
Hollywood to write on the spot. Someone had forgotten to make
accommodations for us (Scott insisted on treating this as a symbol

of the writer's importance in Hollywood), and the only space available was a servant's room under the eaves with a double-deck wire bed. Scott stretched out on his back in the lower, and I in the upper, according to our rank, and we tried to ad-lib a story for the picture which a large and eager camera crew were already on hand to shoot. But the prospect of still another college musical was hardly inspiring, and soon we were comparing the Princeton of his generation with the Dartmouth of mine. I was amazed at the deadly accuracy with which he dissected a campus he had not revisited in years, and in his criticism of an educational system that tends (with certain notable exceptions) to make men conform rather than challenge established ideas I recognized much of the thinking that made *This Side of Paradise* the first and perhaps the only novel that pierces the thin, polished surface of American college life.

Scott was pleased, almost childishly pleased, that I even remembered the book. He seemed surprised that anyone should still consider *The Great Gatsby* a great novel. He was grateful to hear that there were some who found the finest writing of his career in his most recent book, *Tender Is the Night*. He began to talk about himself with frightening detachment. "You know, I used to have a beautiful talent once, Baby. It used to be a wonderful feeling to know it was there, and it isn't all gone yet. I think I have enough left to stretch out over two more novels. I may have to stretch it a little thin, so maybe they won't be as good as the best things I've done. But they won't be completely bad either, because nothing I ever write can ever be completely bad." That's what I heard when my Dartmouth professor told me that Scott was gone.

Despite the twin ironies that the best book Scott wrote in the twenties had nothing to do with flaming youth, while his most profound (if not his most perfect) work appeared toward the middle of the thirties, my generation thought of F. Scott Fitzgerald as an age rather than as a writer, and when the economic stroke of 1929 began to change the sheiks and flappers into unemployed boys or underpaid girls, we consciously and a little belligerently turned our backs on Fitzgerald. We turned our backs on many things.

Some protested they could not read him. I remember arguing with a well read, intelligent Dartmouth footballer who refused to see anything in *Gatsby*. Being serious-minded and a little self-righteous, he seemed to be transferring his contempt for the frivolous waste of the twenties to that amazing little book that seems to catch and hold more of the spirit of that time in two hundred pages than do all the almanacs and Mark Sullivans.

Some had never heard of him. Which recalls an anecdote. Scott had a favorite movie star. One day a friend of his met her on the set and thought she might like to know this. "Scott Fitzgerald," she mused, "I *know* I've heard that name somewhere," and then she remembered. "Oh, I know—isn't he a character in a Katherine Brush novel?" Scott liked his posterity as well as the next man, but this struck his sense of comedy, especially, as he pointed out, since Miss Brush liked to consider herself one of his disciples.

Some thought he was dead. One day several years ago my producer called me in, said he was throwing out my script and putting a new writer on with me. When he told me who it was, I was dumbfounded. "F. Scott Fitzgerald," I said. "I thought he was dead." "If he is," cracked the producer, "he must be the first ghost who ever got $1,500 a week."

I thought he was dead because the era which he had exploited, and which had exploited him, was dead. When I got to know Scott better I discovered that my first reaction had not been entirely true, but neither was it entirely false. When the twenties died, something in Scott died too. But in the way nature compensates a blind man by heightening the sensitivity of his touch, Scott seemed to be developing new values to replace the ones he lost or threw away. Contrary to the critics who have been trying to give him a fast count, *Tender Is the Night* reveals a deeper understanding of human behavior than anything he had done before. And contrary to the premature mourners who had declared him intellectually dead, Scott seemed to be making a conscious, almost a desperate effort to fill the gap in his social observation that prompted Peter Monro Jack to say that a more incisive understanding of the society and times he described so well might have made him the Proust of his generation.

So Scott ends with another great waste to place beside all his other wastes. And now it seems almost too contrived that Scott should have chosen this year in which to die. For it is altogether fitting that Scott's career should begin where one world war ends and end where another begins. He spoke for a new generation that was shell-shocked without ever going to the front. He was one of our better historians of the no-man's-time between wars. He was not meant, temperamentally, to be a cynic, in the same way that beggars who must wander through the cold night were not born to freeze. But Scott made cynicism beautiful, poetic, almost an ideal. There is a line in *This Side of Paradise,* published in 1920, that becomes the epitaph of a postwar generation already being metamorphosed into a pre-(new) war generation:

"I think the worst thing to contemplate is this—it's all happened before, how soon will it happen again?"

—1941

FROM

THE DISENCHANTED

BY BUDD SCHULBERG

In 1950 Budd Schulberg published The Disenchanted, *a roman
à clef about his memorable association with F. Scott Fitzgerald
(described in the previous selection). The just-out-of-college Schulberg
and the novelist past his prime collaborated on the screenplay for
the 1939 film* Winter Carnival *(here titled* Love on Ice; *Fitzgerald
is called Manley Halliday, while Schulberg is Shep Stearns and
Victor Milgrim is famed Hollywood producer Walter Wanger).*

MANLEY HALLIDAY was reading the scenario when Shep
entered. He did not look up until they came half way
across the room to him, and when he did Shep saw an
old young face with ashen complexion. Could this be Manley
Halliday?

Halliday lifted himself out of the deep red leather chair with
stiff good manners. Shep was surprised to see that the author was
several inches shorter than the image in his mind, not much over
five six, a slender, delicately made man with the beginning of small
paunch.

"Glad to meet you, sir," Shep heard himself say under his
breath. But the soft hand hurriedly withdrawn, the disinterested

flick of the eyes drew the meaning of the words.

Shep's own response embarrassed him even though he was helpless to temper it. "It's a great pleasure to meet *you*, Mr. Halliday."

"Manley, it turns out he's one of your fans," Milgrim said
with a laugh.

Shep felt he was being offered up to Manley Halliday. He
wished Milgrim had waited for him to tell Halliday in his own way.

Halliday acknowledged the compliment with an almost
imperceptible bow and the faintest suggestion of a smile, reflect-
ing disbelief rather than pleasure.

"Manley, I thought I'd keep young Stearns on to collaborate
with you—if that's all right with you, of course . . ."

Shep had never seen Milgrim hide his own positiveness under
so much deference. Even the way he said *Manley* seemed to imply
not a casual familiarity but a respectful request for permission to
call him Manley. The first time Shep heard it, he thought Milgrim
had gone out of character. But then he realized that Manley
Halliday was a celebrity from another world, to be admired like
Baruch and Lamont and Einstein. Crawford and Hitchcock and
Cary Grant were the everyday commodities of Milgrim's world.
But Manley Halliday, even ten years late, even on the skids, was a
self-made businessman-artist's ideal of eloquence, of literacy raised
to the level of Pulitzer Prizes and Modern Library editions.

Manley Halliday's *collaborator*. When Milgrim made the suggestion, Shep tried to meet the author's eyes and smile to signal
his realization of the preposterousness of the idea. But Halliday
was polite, in that mannered way associated with capes and walk-
ing sticks, in that way which leaves one totally incapable of per-
ceiving the intention behind the social mask.

"I haven't collaborated with anybody since—Lord, since my
roommate and I wrote the Hasty Pudding show of Fifteen."

He paused, and then added, with what Shep feared was reluc-
tance, "But I'll be glad to try it with Mr. Stearns."

Shep noticed for the first time how Halliday talked. The words came up out of a face that paid no attention to them. Only what had to be said was said. It was said nicely, with a care for amenities, yet accompanied by the unspoken hope that what had just been said would suffice.

In a delayed take—as Milgrim would have said—the producer seemed to realized the incongruity of teaming Halliday with young Stearns, for he hastened to explain, "You may find writing for the movies a little different from your novels, Manley. Most of our writers, even some of the big playwrights, find it easier to have someone for a sounding board." Sensitive to the possible effect of this on Shep's morale, Milgrim added, "And then if there's anything I don't like I can always blame young Stearns here."

Milgrim placed his hand on Shep's shoulder and squeezed it gently to emphasize the good nature of the little joke. But Shep was still too overcome at finding a dead god transformed into a live colleague to care whether he was called collaborator, copy boy or male stenographer. He had even forgotten to worry about the suspended sentence his script apparently had received. All he could think of just then was that he was to have an opportunity to know Manley Halliday, talk to him about his work and discuss the Twenties toward which he felt this incomprehensible nostalgia.

"Well, if everything's all right with you, Manley, I'll leave you two geniuses to work out how you want to get started," Milgrim said, cheerfully managing to pay homage to Halliday on one knee while having his fun at Shep's expense with the other. "Manley, we'd like you to come for dinner soon. Maud will call you. And by the way she's dying to have you autograph your books for her. She's a great collector of autographed books. And she's always said you and Louie Bromfield are her favorite American authors."

Halliday had answered Milgrim with another little dip of his head and a muttered something about being delighted of course.

When Milgrim left them alone they looked at each other—a little guiltily, Shep thought. Why did scenarists so often get that feeling of fellow conspirators?

"I'm afraid I haven't quite finished your script. I'm a very slow reader."

Shep wanted to tell Halliday that the script wasn't really worth his time, that it was just a routine college musical written on order. But then he remembered, almost with a start, that Halliday was being hired to work on *Love on Ice*. Halliday was being paid to read *Love on Ice*. Shep wondered why. He wondered what could have happened to Halliday that would bring him down to this.

He watched Halliday's face as the author supported his head with his thumb to his cheek and two fingers pressed against his forehead. A familiar pose, Shep thought, and then he remembered the jacket of *The Night's High Noon*, when Halliday was the wonder boy of the Twenties, the triple-threat Merriwell of American letters, less real than the most romantic of his heroes, the only writer who could win the approval of Mencken and Stein and make fifty thousand a year doing it and look like Wally Reid. From the rear flap of that book, Shep remembered the exquisite chiseling of the face, the theatrically perfect features, the straight, classical nose, the mouth so beautiful as to suggest effeminacy, the fine forehead, the slicked-down hair parted in the middle. Only an extra delicacy, a refined quality of sensitivity (was it the faint look of amusement uncorrupted by self-satisfaction about the eyes?) marked the difference between that face on the flap and the favorite face of the period. Strange, Shep thought, how faces pass in and out of style like fashions in clothes. The style to which Halliday belonged was the magazine illustration's, the matinee idol's and the movie star's in 1925, the sleek, shiny, Arrow-Collar perfection, finely etched, sharp-featured, a prettyboy face drawn with the symmetry of second-rate art, pear-shaped, with a straight nose, cleft chin, dark hair parted smartly down the middle, combed back and plastered down with Vaseline or sta-comb, the face of someone who has just stepped out of a Turkish bath miraculously recovered from the night before, the clean-cut face of the American sheik, the smoothie, the face of the young sophisticate who has gone places and done things, yet a face curiously unlived in, the face of Neil Hamilton, the face Doug Fairbanks could never quite conceal behind his gay moustaches and Robin Hood's cap, the face Harold Lloyd parodied, that Ramon Navarro and Valentino gave slinky, south-of-the-border imitations of; this was the face of the Twenties, turned in now on a newer, more durable model as befitted more spartan times, but still worn by Manley Halliday like a favorite suit that has not only passed out of style but has worn too thin even for a tailor to patch. The bone structure was still there to remind you of the days when women admirers pasted rotogravure pictures of him inside their copies of his books as others prized photos of John Gilbert and Antonio Moreno. But the hair, still combed back though parted on the side now, was gray and thinning; the famous turquoise eyes had washed out to a milky nondescript; the skin had lost color and tone; the face that Stieglitz had photographed, Davidson had sculptured and Derain painted with such flattering verisimilitude had lost its luster. The association pained Shep but he suddenly thought of the famous juvenile of the Twenties he had seen on the lot the day before, whose receding hairline and expanding waist-line could not alter the fact that he would be a juvenile, irreprievably, until he died.

Reading very slowly, as though reading were a physical effort, the turning of a page a challenge to his strength, Halliday finished the script. Then he read the last page again, stalling for time.

"Well, Stearns, I don't suppose you expect to win any Academy Awards with this but" (Shep saw the attempt at a smile) "I suppose it could be worse. I think we may be able to make a nice little valentine out of it."

But this was the last thing Shep wanted to talk about with Manley Halliday.

"Mr. Halliday, if we stay here and talk, Milgrim'll think we're standing by and grab us for a conference. He seems to be queer for these early-morning conferences. So what do you say we go catch a drink somewhere?"

That was as casual as he could make it; he was eager for the answer.

"I'm not drinking any more."

Halliday wished he had put it less revealingly. To correct the impression, he added hurriedly: "Diabetes. Doctor's orders."

"Then how about a spot of coffee?"

Halliday saw the interest in the young man's eyes.

"Well, I should have been in bed hours ago—more doctor's orders, but maybe one cup of coffee—a quick cup of coffee," he amended. He took a childish—or was it an author's—pride in being able to talk the language of this new generation.

"Swell. How about the Derby?"

"Don't they close at two?"

"Just the bar. I think we can still get in if we move fast."

Shep reached the Derby entrance at least five minutes before Halliday. Two newsboys, a legless veteran and a paralytic, guarded the entrance like deformed sentries. Halliday drove up in an ancient Lincoln roadster. Vintage '33 or '34, Shep pegged it. What's he doing with that beat-up old wreck? The paint had faded, one fender was crumpled and the motor obviously labored under difficulties.

Halliday came toward him out of the darkness of the parking lot and Shep saw why he seemed so out of place here in Beverly Hills; his appearance made no concessions to local fashions. He wore a dark wool overcoat, much too heavy even for the brisk California nights, and a gray homburg. He looked like Fifth Avenue, around the Plaza, on a snappy Sunday afternoon. The image of a ghost came back to Shep as he watched Halliday approach in the pale blur of the street lamps. The ghost goes west, he thought irreverently. Then eagerness hurried him forward.

"Well, did you think I wasn't going to make it? The Smithsonian's been trying to get that bus away from me for years."

It was forced gaiety, delivered with that forced smile that was beginning to make Shep feel uncomfortable.

The Derby was almost empty. Just a few stragglers, a middle-aged man whose face was no match for his sporty clothes, with a very young showgirl, and two men in their middle thirties whom Shep recognized as a successful writing team.

They couldn't help watching their waitress's legs as she strode toward the kitchen. With those Derby get-ups, you had no choice. They wore brown starched hooped skirts that fell short of the knee. It wasn't graceful or becoming and it certainly wasn't practical—just a little public exhibition thrown in with the service. The costumes always bothered Shep. It wasn't like these places he had heard about on the Rue Pigalle where they didn't wear anything at all. At least that was out in the open. This was American sex, awkward and self-conscious and cautiously obscene.

Shep was wondering what Halliday was thinking about.

"Have you worked out here a long time, Stearns? You seem to know your way around."

"This is my first writing job. But I've lived here all my life."

"You mean Hollywood's your home town?" Halliday was mildly interested. "That must have been quite an experience."

Halliday had the typical outsider's view of Hollywood. Though now that Shep thought about it, that wasn't too surprising. One of the weaknesses of *Shadow Ball*—for all its brilliance—had been the inaccuracy of its atmosphere. Not that any single reference had been mistaken—Halliday was too thorough a craftsman for that—it was just that there had been too much atmosphere, too much *Hollywood*, the way one sees it when he's just come in and makes a point of recording all the special things about it, the palm trees, the flamboyancy of the architecture, the jazzed-up mortuaries, the earthquakes, the floods, the pretties on Hollywood Boulevard in their slacks and furs, the million-dollar estates of immigrants who never completely mastered the language of the country they entertain—all these things could be found in Hollywood, but not all run together like that.

"Hollywood was just the name of my home town when I was

a kid," Shep tried to explain. "I raised pigeons, we had gang fights in vacant lots, I ran the 660 for the class B track team at Hollywood High, I sold magazines at Hollywood and Highland, the good-looking girls I knew in school tried to get into the studios the way girls in Lawrence, Mass., tried to get into the textile mills."

"Is your father in the picture business?"

"In a way. He rents cars to studios, all kinds, museum pieces, trucks, break-aways . . . See, that's what I mean, Mr. Halliday. I never thought of Hollywood as anything special at all until I went away to Webster."

"Webster—I used to go up there for football games and parties."

"You did a honey of a job on that flashback to a Webster houseparty in *Friends and Foes,* Mr. Halliday."

So the young man did know something about his books. At least he said he did. Even that was something, these days. "I used to know Webster pretty well. I went up there for a houseparty one fall and stayed until Christmas vacation."

For the first time in years Halliday thought of Hank Osborne, in whose room in the Psi U house he had spent those six crazy weeks. It had been in Hank's room at three o'clock in the morning that they had both decided to quit school and join the Canadian Air Force. Hank had become one of the first celebrated American flyers. After he was shot down and grounded, they had had some high times together in Paris. Hank had written the first sensitive account of a flyer's experiences, done a little painting, married Mignon, contributed to *transition* and helped edit it for a while— then had come that horrendous night—it almost seemed in his life the inevitable night—of the fight: my God, he couldn't even remember *touching* Minnie . . . Years later he had heard that Hank was back at Webster teaching European literature or something.

"You didn't happen to know an instructor called Osborne up there? Hank Osborne?"

"Professor Osborne! Sure, I had him in Modern French Literature. A swell Joe. And terrific on Zola and Balzac. He was head of our chapter of the League Against War and Fascism when I was up there."

Yes, Halliday remembered Hank's going left. Back from Paris in Thirty-one, out of a job, out of money and, even more serious, out of a way of life, there probably hadn't seemed any other place for Hank to go.

"Professor Osborne's a great admirer of yours, Mr. Halliday."

So Hank hadn't let these years—Lord, was it more than ten!—of bad feeling influence his opinion of Manley's work. Well, that was pretty decent of Hank, more than he might have expected. After all, in those good years on the continent, Hank had been mighty jealous of his success. The time he accepted Hank's invitation to tell him *exactly* what he thought of his novel, for instance, the one that never got published—*that's* what it had really been about, not the silly drunken business of Mignon.

"Well, I'm glad to hear I still have a few boosters."

Halliday had meant it to pass for modesty. He was a little dismayed himself at the tone of self-pity that accompanied it. This had happened several times recently and he must guard against it. There must be no more of this going around to the back door begging complimentary handouts.

"Mr. Halliday, I might as well jump in with both feet. I've read all your books. *High Noon* was the closest thing to a Bible I had in college. There used to be a group of us at Webster who'd sit around quoting Halliday to each other."

"Is that so?"

Shep saw a flicker of interest in Halliday's eyes.

"I know it sounds kind of—grandiose, but our whole intellectual attitude toward the war and the Twenties was based more than anything else on *Friends and Foes* and *The Night's High Noon*. Gee, Keith Winters, Ted Bentley and those other characters of yours, we knew them so well they were almost like roommates."

Halliday was listening intently. Shep hurried on.

"I really felt I was living through the Twenties with Ted

Bentley. He was such a terrific symbol of the conflicting values of the times, the corrosive materialism. And yet he wasn't a symbol. Not a theory dressed up as a man like Charley Anderson in *U.S.A.* Bentley lives in your book. Sometimes in school I'd find myself arguing about various attitudes typical of the Twenties as if I had actually been around in those days and experienced them myself. And then I'd realize it was actually Ted Bentley's experiences, Ted's attitudes I had lived my way into."

This kind of enthusiasm could not be fabricated. Halliday's ego was warmed as surprisingly as if one were to go out for a night's stroll and discover the sun. He often found himself slipping into the vain third-person: nobody reads Halliday any more. The year before last he had written his publisher suggesting a one-volume collected Halliday to reintroduce him to the new readers of the Thirties. And Burt Seixas, his old friend, his discoverer, had given him that old run-around: "Now doesn't seem to be quite the right time" . . . Maybe after they published that "new" novel Manley had been promising ever since *Shadow Ball* . . . But here, from a most unexpected source, was what he was hungering for—proof of the lasting value of his work.

"I'm honestly surprised my books stay with you this way. They were written so long ago, in such a different time. I had the idea your generation went in more for Steinbeck and Farrell and Tom Wolfe. The holy trinity!"

Though the remark was dusted with sarcasm, Shep's earnestness brushed it off. "I think Steinbeck's the kind of writer we've needed in the Thirties, maybe the best we've got who's producing at the moment . . ."

Shep was too wound up to notice the slur or its effect on Halliday.

"—at least he tries to deal honestly with the depression. With people, I mean working people. You know what Ralph Fox says—the only class that can still produce heroes."

Because each was willing to accept the other as representative

of his time, they stepped gingerly over the lines of disagreement
into the area of common understanding.

"How long has it been since you've read *High Noon*,
Stearns?"

"I know this sounds phony, but I read it again just a couple of
weeks ago. That girl you've got in there, Lenore Woodbury, she
fascinates me. That's a great scene, really a terrific scene, when she
calls Ted up at the Club after he's left her and tells him what a wise
move she thinks this is for him, how she realizes she can't help
making a mess of everything she touches because she's sick inside
with the incurable sickness of the times—and all the while Ted has
his bag packed ready to come back to her. And then it almost drives
him nuts trying to figure out whether she called him to get him
back or to strengthen his will to stay away."

"Poor Lenore didn't know herself."

"That's the way you make us feel about your characters—that
no one is forcing them to do anything—that they're living, trying
to make up their own minds from page to page."

"I guess that's the hardest part, trying to keep your long arm
out of your characters' way."

"I suppose everybody asks you this, Mr. Halliday, but was
Lenore a real person—someone you actually knew?"

As if awakening from a long sleep, the loneliness in him stirred
to find her again—Jere . . . Jere . . . Calling into a void, into nothing, nothingness, and the only answer was the muffled echo jeer-
ing *ree-ree-ree* . . . It was a buzzing in his ears, a familiar symptom.

"Mr. Halliday, are you all right?"

"Yes—yes—these late hours. Better get our check."

While they waited for their change, Halliday braced himself.
He had a strong sense of pattern, and since this had been a good
evening he did not want to let it down. "Well, we didn't accom-
plish too much with *Love on Ice*—except to break the ice a little bit
ourselves. But, this has been rather pleasant. When I think of some
of the collaborators I might have drawn . . ."

"I've still got a million things to ask you about your work. I hope you don't mind."

"Not at all, not at all. I'm delighted to find a young man seriously interested in literature—especially my own."

Shep grinned when he saw the quick light that brightened Halliday's face—his first spontaneous smile of the evening.

Halliday was in his car now. "Well, Stearns, I'd better get home and start catching up on my sleep. I've read somewhere that the secret of screen-writing is a sound mind in a sound body."

The smile was meant to be as genuine as the one that preceded it, but something began to go wrong with it. It proved to be a dud and fizzled out.

What time should they meet next morning? Say around ten, Shep suggested. Halliday's creative juices weren't used to flowing much before noon, but he'd try. Anything to please a gentleman and a collaborator, and, most important of all, Halliday added with a little flourish, "a loyal reader."

He touched the homburg in a dignified—and to Shep strangely old-fashioned—gesture of farewell.

Shep stood there watching while the old Lincoln moved slowly down the whole boulevard. When it was almost out of sight a hopped-up Ford with a gaga passenger list of three high-school couples came up fast on the outside and let the Lincoln have it with one of those comical horns that play *My-dog-has-fleas*. Halliday cut sharply to the curb and proceeded at an even slower pace until Shep lost him in the fog of the street lights.

MY BOSS, SCOTT FITZGERALD

BY FRANCES KROLL RING

Frances Kroll Ring worked as F. Scott Fitzgerald's assistant from the spring of 1939 until his death in December 1940. The first piece here appeared in 1964 in Los Angeles *magazine; the second, which is an excerpt from a longer article, comes from a 1959 issue of* Esquire. *Ring also published a book about her Fitzgerald experience,* Against the Current: As I Remember F. Scott Fitzgerald *(1985).*

APPARENTLY, THE READING public is not yet sated by all that has been written about the shining but ill-fated talent of F. Scott Fitzgerald. Just the other evening, I received a phone call from a man who introduced himself as a collector of Fitzgerald-lore. He had recently come to Los Angeles to teach and since I was among those present in the final act of Fitzgerald's dramatic life, he hoped I might be able to add to his collection.

Fitzgerald's story has been dealt with in an increasing number of good books and articles. But the inquisitors keep seeking. It is as if they were expecting some yet unrevealed hint that would explain why a man so richly endowed should have had the discouraging experience of losing both his audience and his golden promise during his lifetime.

And so again, I find myself looking back through the filmy distance of twenty-odd years for some clue to the fascination Fitzgerald still excites in new generations of readers.

It was in the Spring of 1939 that I went to work for Scott Fitzgerald as his personal secretary. He was living in a rambling cottage in Encino, and though he was dressed in an old bathrobe over an old sweater, he had an air of charm and graciousness that belied his outfit. Once it was established that I had the technical ability to fill the job, his chief concern was whether or not I was "trustworthy" for he was planning to write a novel about Hollywood and he wanted it kept very confidential.

I assured him that I was reared in the Lincoln tradition, but Fitzgerald had to prove it in his own way. Casually, he asked me to open a bureau drawer. It was filled with gin bottles. I neither expressed horror, nor ran from the room. He then gave me some cash—about $35—and asked me to go to a Western Union office and wire the money to his daughter in Poughkeepsie. When this was done, I was to phone him. Of course, if I made off with the money and didn't call or come back, then I couldn't be trusted. It was like a child's game. I passed the oversimplified character test and thus began a mutually respectful and unforgettable relationship.

As the bureau drawer indicated, he was on a detour into partial oblivion, having just returned from a visit to his wife, Zelda. Contact with the sick remains of a once vital love invariably drove him to the anesthesia of drink. He made a great pretense of keeping his drinking secret so that word would not get around to the studios and put him on the alcoholic blacklist. Only once while I worked for him did he get involved in a bar incident. This ended disastrously. The next morning the George Street Receiving Hospital called me to come and get him. He was quiet and abashed all the way home. This was a depth he had not meant to fathom.

Was he kidding himself? Not at all. Despite his condition, he retained at all times an innate dignity and self respect and made continuous efforts to keep a part of himself intact and functioning for some hours each day. As a result, I was often as caught up doing mundane chores as I was intrigued by his lively personality.

The chores were anything from marketing; rummaging in book stores for good used copies of books he considered classics; examining old newspaper files in the public library for information about motion picture personalities for his planned novel (*The Last Tycoon*); reading to him from "Ecclesiastes"; opening a can of turtle soup for his lunch; to filling a gunny sack with empty gin bottles and dropping them over the side of a canyon so that his consumption would not be revealed to the trash snoopers, whoever they might be.

When he had had enough of this busy work, and when his bank account reached a danger point, he had the miraculous will to redirect his energies to his craft. Although periodically unsure of his ability to sell his work, the process of getting something down on paper each day had a revivifying effect on his confidence in his ability to write.

It was to "Pat Hobby," leading character of a series of stories born out of this last period, that Fitzgerald transferred much of his antagonism toward the Hollywood system for writers, though any similarity between Fitzgerald and the fictional hack, Pat Hobby, is strictly in the realm of imagination.

Fitzgerald worked at the studios only occasionally, but still at top prices. More often than not, he revitalized another writer's tired script. There was a week at Goldwyn's on *Raffles*. He worked right on the set repairing dialogue for David Niven and Olivia de Havilland as the picture was being shot. The rush was due to the fact that Niven was going off to war and there would be no time to shoot and repair later. The job hardly challenged Fitzgerald— he did it, as usual, for the money—but he was fascinated by the dash and courage of Niven, the handsome warrior, a role Fitzgerald had visualized but never achieved in his own youthful war experience.

Another studio job was at 20th Century Fox. One September morn, we arrived armed with a briefcase filled with Coca-Cola.

This was before the days of Coke machines and Fitzgerald needed the stimulus of this soft drink to keep him energized throughout what turned out to be long, tedious days. He laughed at the advertising possibilities of this Coke-in-a-briefcase idea and then waited and waited and waited in offices in the Writers Building. Fitzgerald made himself comfortable by taking off his shoes (tight shoes made him quarrel with producers, he said) and kept busy writing letters throughout the long, silent day until word might come from above. Above meant Zanuck. Finally, with the day gone, he urged me to go home. There was not much point in hanging around. He would get in touch with me as soon as he had some definite word about the assignment.

It wasn't until early the next morning that I was awakened by Western Union. The message read: "HIGHLY SUCCESSFUL CONFERENCE FROM 11 TO 1(AM). PLEASE BE AT OFFICE BY TEN TWENTY TO HOLD FORT BUT DON'T PHONE ME UNLESS HEADQUARTERS CALL. A THOUSAND WILD STORMY KISSES (signed) TYRONE."

(Tyrone Power was, of course, 20th's favorite son at the time and I could hardly resent being awakened, no matter what the hour, by a combination of Tyrone and Fitzgerald.)

After about three weeks, Fitzgerald was free. He went home again to "Pat Hobby" whose dissolute antics, while less remunerative than screen writing, nonetheless amused him and helped pay the rent so that he could tackle *The Last Tycoon*, a novel of the motion picture industry on a grand scale—of the struggle between the creative and financial forces that masterminded the industry rather than of the peripheral hangers-on like Pat.

Fitzgerald's working habits were extraordinarily methodical for a man thought to be "finished," or by some, even "dead." He threw himself into this project with the abandon of a writer who knew where he was going all the way, sifting notes, arranging them, rearranging them, and then with the inevitable irony that plagued him throughout his life, he suffered a serious heart attack. He was ordered to bed but he could not rest. With a bed desk perched across his lap, he worked intensely for several hours each day, determined to finish the book that would put him in print again; fighting all the time against the deadline of his weakened heart until it gave out . . .

The aura of enchantment that re-emblazoned his name upon his death in December 1940 was ironic. His lost decade was retrieved and dusted off. In the thirties, the realistic bread and butter issues of the times out-shouted him. The emotional depression he concerned himself with at a time when the country was experiencing an economic depression fell on unsympathetic intellects. But by the early forties, there was a new and receptive audience with full stomachs and rumbling psyches. They were attuned to emotional anguish and could relate to this esthetic, romantic writer who had suffered and described the heights as well as the deepest despair of love both in his own life and in his work.

When the unfinished *Last Tycoon* was published, critics almost unanimously doffed their hats. It revealed a breadth of talent that was his final vindication. To those who thought him frivolous, he proved himself serious; to those who had thought he lacked social conscience, he showed a comprehension of the forces of labor and management at work in the movie industry; to those who had, on occasion, accused him of anti-Semitism, his studio "bad man" had no Semitic taint. And, in addition, he was capable of creating an exquisite love story. That measure of immortality he so wanted to achieve was his.

There is no doubt that he had a premonition of death and this simple incident reveals something of the practical side of the man. One day, he told me that he had put about $700 in cash in his top bureau drawer. He wanted me to know about the money so that if anything happened to him, I could make the proper arrangements without bucking the complications of a tied-up checking account.

I tried to dismiss his fearful precaution, hoping it was just a further extension of his usual hypochondria—but as it turned out, this time his fears were well founded. Before the year was out, it was necessary to use the money for the most difficult thing he had ever asked me to do . . .

The gentle voice had now been silenced, the lively mind put at rest. What remained of this once-romantic figure, whose health had been recklessly dissipated by the time he was forty, was a lost decade of his reputation to be retrieved, dusted off and reestablished. Left behind, also, were the scattered remnants of his family. Despite the separation of miles and illness, he had been the apex of the Scott, Scottie and Zelda triangle, giving it support, advice, discipline (oft-times severe) and direction.

In August of 1940, he wrote to Scottie, "I have always hoped life would throw you among lawyers or men who were going into politics or big time journalism. They lead rather larger lives." It is rather interesting to observe that whether she did it consciously or not, Scottie married a lawyer and has been involved in a "bigger life" in and around Washington.

As for Zelda, he left her "bereft of the happy haven of a heart that cared" and wanting some memento, like his "old worn Thesaurus."

Scottie, too, wrote me and asked for "something of his like a pen knife or paper weight" not for herself but for a devoted friend, Mrs. Turnbull, whose son Andrew has since become Fitzgerald's biographer and whose edition of Fitzgerald's letters (a current bestseller), speaks for itself—eloquently.

What manner of man was this that a souvenir could be so meaningful to those who knew him so well, and had their private memories to refer to? Without deifying the image of Fitzgerald, it must be said that he genuinely cared about people, and was ever absorbed with the problems of his family and friends. And while the pressure that resulted from this concern undoubtedly created a private torment for him, causing him to behave diabolically and distracting him from the level of achievement he wanted to attain, it may well have given dimension to his personality. Certainly it left its imprint on those close to him. His last love, Sheilah Graham, observed, "He had taught me that every human being has value."

Though in later years some of Fitzgerald's lustre had faded, his "scape-grace wit and disarming grace," as poet John Bishop called it, were still there. As for the promise, it too was once again in evidence, but—true to the pattern of his life—interrupted by final tragedy.

—1964

P ERIODICALLY, I'M asked questions about him. Perhaps a few answers may round out the existing picture of him:

What did he look like? He was handsome, but faded, except for the bright blue of his eyes. His clothes had seen better days. He didn't indulge in a wardrobe until just a few months before his death when he bought a Brooks Brothers suit, and was as delighted with his purchase as a child with a treat. One might say he gave the appearance of impoverished gentility. However, his personal charm remained undiminished even though it was no longer fashionably set off.

Did he drink? When I first came to work for him, in the Spring of 1939, he kept a water tumbler by his side. I soon learned that the tumbler was a deceptive gin container. When the economic pressure became insistent, however, he was able to cut down on his consumption and get to work. More often than not, he substituted enormous quantities of Coca-Cola. His limited energy demanded the stimulation of a drink or a Coke to get him through his work. He was a private drinker and rarely belligerent. His chief anger was directed against his "agents" whom he damned for *their* inability to get him work. He kept his sense of humor always. Once when I relayed a message that a "Mr. Batt had phoned" he replied, "Must be my old friend On a Bat."

He was reluctant to acknowledge his alcoholism and in writing to family or friends invariably made reference to being bedded, or running temperatures. Certainly it is not for us to pass moral judgment on a man for his private habits, especially when, even in his dreariest moments, his familial responsibilities were not neglected. No matter what his condition, he maintained his position as head of three households—his daughter at school, his wife in a sanitarium and his own semblance of home.

Drink for the sake of drink was not his area of decline, only a manifestation of it. He resorted to excess when his emotional or creative wells ran a dry spell. If any one thing can be said to be the cause of his periods of self-destruction, it was rather the tragic quality of his love.

What were his working habits? A self-imposed whip drove him to some hours of work each day. He could not afford to be idle. Once the material was organized in his mind, he wrote quickly. He set very high standards for himself and fortunately he had the originality and creativity to achieve them. But his concern with minor corrections, once a story had gone out to a publication, indicates a certain unsureness of acceptance. Sometimes, the revisions were hardly more than a word or two on a given page which in no way affected the story, but seemed to relieve some desperate, perfectionist standard of his own. He wrote his stories in longhand on legal-size paper, then had triple-spaced drafts typed for corrections and revisions. He dictated letters and screen plays, pacing back and forth as he dramatically uttered the dialogue.

How did he live? He lived very simply. Outside of attending movie previews, books, music and talk filled his quiet evenings at home. He loved to talk and shared his opinions with anyone who would listen to him. He was warm and kind to the people who worked for him and had a rather nice way of showing it. For instance, he was a great football fan. One night when Kenny Washington was playing for UCLA, he insisted upon taking his Negro cook and her husband to the game because he felt they should see this all-time great player. Then there was an incident when he had to release his housekeeper from service because he could no longer afford full-time help. When he discovered she was going to have a baby, he continued her salary for a few weeks, though he was scraping the bottom of the barrel.

He had, of course, a writer's curiosity. He was always asking questions about my background and family. When he learned that my father's old-world education had consisted of learning the Bible from memory, he promptly sent him a copy of a New Testament with the inscription:

For Samuel Kroll from a friend and collaborator of his daughter's hoping that whether or not he agrees with this modern way of translating scripture, it may give him some interest to glance over it.

—*F. Scott Fitzgerald, Encino, 1939*

His essential character is most beautifully summed up by his wife, Zelda, in a letter to me after his death.

Dear Miss Kroll: Again, I express my gratitude to you for your kindness to my husband. Though I knew that he was ill, his death was a complete shock to me, and so heartbreaking that I am inadequate to his last necessity for me.

My husband did so much for other people. Many nights I have known him to sit up over another manuscript when his own was not completed; and one of my most happy memories are the times he spent lost in interest and enthusiasm for the work of a prospective author.

He was generous spiritually as he was materially and I am sure that he left many friends behind. . . .

I am grateful that I still have my daughter. Life is almost unendurably sad without the inalienable ties that soften its inescapable tragedies.

That's why I feel even worse that my husband should have died out there alone and am so reiterant about the appreciation of your sympathy and efforts.

With kindest regards, Zelda Fitzgerald

—*1959*

BELOVED INFIDEL

BY SHEILAH GRAHAM

These excerpts from Sheilah Graham's 1958 autobiography detail her three-year relationship with F. Scott Fitzgerald. When the two first met in Hollywood in July 1937, Graham was a well-known syndicated gossip columnist and engaged to the Marquess of Donegall, an English aristocrat, and Fitzgerald was eking out a living writing screenplays. Although their union was not alto-gether happy—Fitzgerald's drinking caused many rifts—their bond was deep.

IT BEGAN AT MY HOUSE high in the Hollywood hills, which I'd rented a few weeks before. [Robert] Benchley lent me his German boy to serve. Donegall and I were toasted in cham-pagne, and I wandered happily among my guests—Eddie Mayer, Frank Morgan, Lew Ayres, Charlie Butterworth, writers and actors and their wives and girls. From my little terrace the lights of Hollywood far below gleamed and flickered like tiny paper lanterns strung through the streets of some distant, festive city floating in the sky. It was a night for dreams.

I clung to Donegall's arm. What more lovely dream of splen-dor could I wish for? The toasts and good healths came fast. Benchley's boy served industriously, we all drank, and amid the laughter and gaiety I heard Bob shout, "Let's all go to my place! Remember the Bastille!"

Noisily we piled into half a dozen cars parked outside and drove down the hill to the Garden of Allah. We trooped into Bob's small drawing room and there was more champagne, and more guests—Dorothy Parker, Alan Campbell, a European actress named Tala Birrell—and the party went on even more merrily. Donegall's arm was around me, Frank Morgan was telling a hilarious story, and almost casually I became aware of blue smoke curling lazily upward in the bright radiance of a lamp. Then I saw a man I had not seen before. He sat quietly in an easy chair under the lamp, and from a cigarette motionless in his hand the blue smoke wafted slowly upward. I stared at him, not sure whether I saw him or not: he seemed unreal, sitting there so quietly, so silently, in this noisy room, watching everything yet talking to no one, no one talking to him—a slight, pale man who appeared to be all shades of the palest, most delicate blue: his hair was pale, his face was pale, like a Marie Laurencin pastel, his suit was blue, his eyes, his lips were blue, behind the veil of blue smoke he seemed an apparition that might vanish at any moment. I turned to laugh with Frank Morgan; Bob spoke to me; when I looked again, the chair was empty. Only the blue smoke remained in the heavy air, curling upon itself as it slowly flowed into the updraft of the lamp. I thought, someone *was* there.

I turned to Bob. "Who was that man sitting under the lamp? He was so quiet."

Bob looked. "That was F. Scott Fitzgerald—the writer. I asked him to drop in." He peered owlishly about the room. "I guess he's left—he hates parties."

"Oh," I said. "I wish I'd known before. I would have liked to talk to him." I thought, he's the writer of the gay twenties, of flaming youth, of bobbed hair and short skirts and crazy drinking—the jazz age. I had even made use of his name: in "Sheilah Graham Says," when I wanted to chide women for silly behavior, I described them as passé, as old-fashioned F. Scott Fitzgerald types, though I had never read anything he wrote. It might have been interesting to talk to him.

A few days later Marc Connolly asked me to a Writers' Guild dinner dance at the Coconut Grove in downtown Los Angeles. He had taken a table for ten; so had Dorothy Parker, chairman of the evening. I don't know how it happened but a moment came when I found myself sitting all alone at our long table, and at Dorothy's table, parallel to ours, sat a man I recognized as Scott Fitzgerald, all alone at his table. We were facing each other. He looked at me almost inquiringly as if to say, I have seen you somewhere, haven't I? and smiled. I smiled back. Seeing him clearly now, I saw that he looked tired, his face was pale, pale as it had been behind the veil of blue smoke that night at Benchley's, but I found him most appealing: his hair pale blond, a wide, attractive forehead, gray-blue eyes set far apart, set beautifully in his head, a straight, sharply chiseled nose and an expressive mouth that seemed to sag a little at the corners, giving the face a gently melancholy expression. He appeared to be in his forties but it was difficult to know; he looked half-young, half-old: the thought flashed through my mind, he should get out into the sun, he needs light and air and warmth. Then he leaned forward and said, smiling across the two tables, "I like you."

I was pleased. Smiling, I said to him, "I like you, too."

There was silence for a moment. This was my first evening out since my engagement and, in a magnificent evening gown of gray with a crimson velvet sash, I felt exquisitely beautiful, as befitted a girl who was to become a marchioness. To be sitting now, alone, while everyone was dancing, seemed such a waste. I said to Mr. Fitzgerald, "Why don't we dance?"

He smiled again, a quick smile that suddenly transfigured his face: it was eager and youthful now, with all trace of melancholy gone. "I'm afraid I promised to dance the next one with Dorothy Parker. But after that—"

But when everyone returned to their tables the band stopped playing; there were many speeches and when they were over everyone scrambled to go home and I did not see him again. Marc Connolly took me home and once more I had brushed against this quiet, attractive man and we had careened off in opposite directions.

Yet something was at work.

I learned a little more about Scott Fitzgerald. He was married but his wife Zelda, a great beauty with whom he was very much in love, was in a mental institution and had been for some time. It was a tragic story. So that, I thought, lies behind the sad line of his mouth, explains the hint of melancholy lurking behind his reserve. From scraps of conversation between Eddie and Bob Benchley, I gathered that Scott and Zelda had lived a rather daring, unconventional life, full of outrageous pranks and escapades. Once they had jumped fully dressed into the fountain in front of the Plaza Hotel in New York. They would hire taxicabs and ride on the hood. I thought to myself, that isn't screamingly funny. I gathered, too, that though Eddie and his friends looked on Scott as a great American writer, nobody paid much attention to him now. People were reading his contemporaries—Ernest Hemingway, Thomas Wolfe, John Steinbeck—while Scott was appearing only now and then in magazines such as *Esquire*.

Tuesday afternoon a telegram arrived from Scott. He could not keep our engagement that evening. His daughter had just arrived from the East and he was taking her to diner. I recall that he had spoken of his fifteen-year-old daughter, Scottie, who attended boarding school in Connecticut. Helen Hayes, a friend of the Fitzgeralds, was bringing her to California on a brief visit. I stared at the telegram, astonished at the intensity of my disappointment. For a moment I was dismayed: how could I be so shaken by this? I was to marry Donegall in six months: how could I be so affected by a broken date with a man—and a married man— whom I had seen for the first time less than ten days ago? Yet suddenly I knew I must see Scott again. Nothing else mattered. I telephoned him. "Scott," I said, "it makes no difference, your daughter being here. I'd like to meet her. Can't we all go to dinner?"

There was a pause. Then, reluctantly, "All right. I'll pick you up at seven."

Scottie was a pretty, vivacious girl with her father's eyes and forehead, which made me like her instantly. Two boys she had known in the East had called and Scott had invited them, too. At dinner, however, Scott was an altogether different man from the charming cavalier who had danced with me. He was tense and on edge: he was continually correcting his daughter unfairly and embarrassingly. "Scottie, finish your meat," and "Scottie, don't touch your hair," and "Scottie, sit up straight." She endured it patiently but now and then she turned on him with a despairing, "Oh, Daddy, please—" As the evening progressed Scott grew increasingly nervous, drumming on the table, lighting one cigarette from another, and drinking endless Coca-Colas. It was obvious that he loved his daughter but he fussed about her unbearably. My heart went out to Scottie who would sit there, silently, and sigh as if to say, why doesn't he stop it? Then she and the boys would fall to giggling, only to have Scott interrupt with a heavily jovial story which they apparently found not funny at all. Scott and I danced a few times but he was distracted and worried. The evening was a strain for everyone. I thought, is this the man I found so fascinating? This anxious, middle-aged father? It was a relief when he said to his daughter, "Scottie, don't you think it's time for you to be in bed? I ought to take you back to the hotel." We dropped the boys off, then dropped Scottie at the hotel where she was staying with Miss Hayes, and Scott took me to my home on the hill.

He stood at the door, saying good-bye. I felt utterly lonely and on the point of tears. There had been such a magical quality about him the other night and now he was only a faded little man who was a father. He said good night. I did not want him to go; I felt inexpressibly sad that something that had been so enormously exciting and warming had gone. I thought, oh, what a pity to lose this. In the half light, as he stood there, his face was beautiful. You could not see the tiredness, the grayness, you only saw his eyes, set so beautifully in his head, and the marvelous line from cheekbone to chin. I wanted desperately to recapture the enchantment that had been and I heard myself whisper, "Please don't go, come in," and I drew him in and he came in and as he came in he kissed me and suddenly he was not a father anymore and it was as though this was as it should be, must be, inevitable and foreordained.

I tried to bolster him in my own way. "Scott," I said one evening, "I feel badly. Here you are, a famous writer, and I've not read a thing you've written. I want to read every one of your books."

"Do you really?" he asked, pleased. I discovered that when he spoke of his work he never disparaged it: he spoke of it with great seriousness. It was not a subject for self-deprecation or witticisms. "All right, Sheilo. I'll get you my books. Let's get them tonight." After dinner, we strolled into Hollywood's biggest book store. Scott asked, "Have you books by F. Scott Fitzgerald?"

The clerk, a young man, said, "Sorry—none in stock." He turned inquiringly to another customer.

"Do you have any calls for them?" Scott pursued.

"Oh—once in a while," said the clerk. "But not for some time, now."

I did not look at Scott as we walked out but I said hurriedly, "Let's try another place." It was the same story there. At the third bookstore, a small shop, the owner, a gray-haired man, was on a ladder placing a book on a high shelf. He came down slowly. At Scott's question he shook his head but said, "I believe I can get hold of a title or two. Which ones are you interested in?"

"I'd appreciate that," Scott said, carefully. He gave the names of three: *This Side of Paradise, The Great Gatsby, Tender Is the Night.* The gray-haired man said, "I'll do my best to find these for you."

Scott said, almost diffidently, "I'm Mr. Fitzgerald."

The other's eyes widened. He put out his hand and shook Scott's warmly. "I'm happy to meet you, Mr. Fitzgerald," he said. "I've enjoyed your books very much." He was quite impressed. He took Scott's address. "I'll really get these for you, and if there aren't any about, I'll order them from the publishers."

Scott thanked him and we left the story. I wondered, how must he feel to have been so famous once and almost unknown now—the courteous, self-effacing man who escorted Sheilah Graham to dinners and premieres, but always slipped in the side entrance with her, and always, when introduced to her friends, had to face the same reaction: a widening of the eyes, a smile of surprise as though they were astonished to find that F. Scott Fitzgerald was still alive.

There was so much I did not know about Scott. Salaries in Hollywood are no secret: I learned that he was being paid a thousand dollars a week for the period of his six months' contract. Compared to the hundred and sixty a week John Wheeler was now paying me, this was a fortune. I thought only eccentricity led Scott to ride about in his little second-hand car, and to wear nondescript clothes. Only later was I to learn that he was in debt more than forty thousand dollars, that the cost of Zelda's sanitarium and keeping Scottie in boarding school were tremendous burdens; that more than a year before he had suffered a terrifying breakdown, a period of utter panic in which he thought he would never write again, that drinking had been his demon and his despair; that he had come to Hollywood in a desperate attempt to re-establish himself, hoping to earn enough money to pay his debts and perhaps be enabled to return to serious writing again.

Scott burst in, his eyes dancing with excitement. He had seen a notice in the *Los Angeles Times* that the Pasadena Playhouse was to present the play version of his short story, "A Diamond As Big As The Ritz." We were going to the opening—we'd make a festive occasion of it. Dress in evening clothes, dine at the Trocadero, and go on to Pasadena—not in his bouncy little Ford but in a sleek, chauffeur-driven limousine he'd hire for the night. I was as enthusiastic as Scott. A play based on one of his short stories! And at the Playhouse, which was sometimes a prelude to Broadway!

At the Trocadero, Scott was in excellent humor. He looked dapper in his best white dinner shirt and tuxedo. I wore my gray and crimson evening gown decorated with a lovely corsage he had sent me in honor of the occasion and, very proudly, a silver-fox jacket he had bought for my birthday. This was the first genuine fur piece I had ever possessed. Scott laughed as I sat forward in my seat lest I wear down the fur.

Metro had picked up his option, assuring him an additional twelve months of employment, and he was once more on his Coca-Cola and coffee regimen. We had spent much of our time going to the movies, Scott watching the screen with the rapt attention of a student. He considered motion pictures a powerful medium for the writer: he was determined to master the technique of screen writing. Twice before he had tried his hand at it in Hollywood, in 1927 and 1931, but only briefly.

This time he would really devote himself to the task. He had once studied short stories in the same fashion, he told me, analyzing the plots of a hundred *Saturday Evening Post* stories. Now, at Metro, he had pictures run off daily in order to study them. Hollywood itself—its people and its habits—he found fascinating. The studio had talked to him about writing a new Joan Crawford picture. He told me about it gleefully. "Their first title was

'Infidelity'; now they've changed it to 'Fidelity.'" This amused him. He had been amused, too, by his first meeting with Miss Crawford. Quite humbly he had told her, "I'm going to write your next picture." She had smiled at him. "Good," she had said, fixing him with her burning eyes. "Write hard, Mr. Fitzgerald, write hard!" Scott, telling it, threw back his head and laughed.

He was very interested, he said, as our limousine took us to Pasadena, in the struggle going on between the forces of Irving Thalberg, who died at the age of thirty-seven a year before, and those of Louis B. Mayer. He saw this as a war between art and money, between the unselfish boy genius, represented by Thalberg, and the ruthless industrialist, represented by Mayer. The idea of a novel had been simmering in Scott's mind, he told me, ever since he met Thalberg, on a previous visit to Hollywood. "No one's yet written *the* novel on Hollywood," Scott went on. Until now, most writers had approached Hollywood almost sneeringly, treating it as though it were a cartoon strip peopled by one-dimensional comic-book characters—every producer gross and illiterate, every writer charmingly unstable, every star an over-grown child. Scott would write a serious novel about Hollywood: he would build it around Thalberg, and the struggle for power—the creative versus the commercial, would be its basic theme.

He talked about "A Diamond As Big As The Ritz." He knew that someone had turned it into a play but nothing had come of it. Now that it was being put on by the Playhouse, he began to have hope again. He had telephoned the Playhouse, telling them he was the author of the story, and asked them to reserve two seats for him "somewhere near the back."

Our car drew up before the theater and the chauffeur helped us out. It was strange to see no cars discharging other first nighters, no activity at the box office. "Could I have gotten the date wrong?" Scott asked me, perplexed. With a sinking feeling I waited in the deserted lobby while he went off to find someone. When he returned, his walk wasn't quite as jaunty. "It's the students—they're giving the play in the upstairs hall," he said, trying to be casual. I said nothing as we climbed the stairs and found ourselves in a small hall with a little stage and perhaps fifteen rows of wooden benches. No one else had arrived.

We sat on a bench in the back, waiting, and I tried to chat animatedly of what I had done during the day, to ask countless questions about *Three Comrades*, about the disagreements over the script he had been having with Joe Mankewicz, its producer, about his plans for "Fidelity" or "Infidelity" or whatever its final title would be.

About ten minutes before curtain time a few students arrived, women and girls wearing mostly slacks and skirts—perhaps a dozen in all. They looked curiously at us sitting alone on a bench in full evening clothes. The lights finally went down, the curtain parted, and the play began. It was an amateur performance but Scott laughed while the students giggled and in the end his applause outlasted theirs. They wandered off and we were left alone again. Scott rose. "I'm going backstage," he said. "It might encourage them to know the author came to see them."

He returned a few moments later and we went down the stairs to our waiting limousine. We drove back to Hollywood and did not talk much. At first Scott said, almost cheerfully, "They were all nice kids—they seemed a little awkward when I introduced myself. I told them they'd done a good job." As we rode on, however, despite what chatter I could manage, Scott grew more and more glum, and finally sat silent and depressed next to me. Of course they were awkward, ran through my mind. They were embarrassed to meet a man they had thought dead.

It was a Thursday afternoon in November [1940], a dull, gray day, and I was curled up on the sofa, listening to the massed voices lifted in the stirring chorus of Bach's cantata *Singet dem Herrn*. Then

I looked up. Scott was there, gray and trembling, letting himself slowly into his easy chair. Alarmed, I asked, "Is anything the matter, Scott?" I hurried to turn down the music. He lit a cigarette carefully before he spoke. "I almost fainted at Schwab's," he said. "Everything started to fade." He had never felt quite like that before. "I think I'd better see Dr. Wilson in the morning."

"Scott, I wish you would," I said, thinking, *Scott and his hypochondria*. I tried never to comment on his aches and pains because he was so quick to resent my concern.

In the morning he drove downtown to Dr. Wilson's office. He was back an hour later, his face solemn— He said, "I had a cardiac spasm."

A great pang of fear shot through me. "Is that a heart attack?"

Scott was vague. "No—"

"Did he say you must stay in bed?"

"No," said Scott. He lied, and I did not know. "But I must take it easy. Stairs are out."

I was relieved. Dr. Wilson had not put him to bed. I had read about heart attacks. If you had one, you were sent to bed at once and kept there, flat on your back. Yet Scott must take care of himself. His apartment was on the third floor, mine on the first. "All right," I said. "You move in with me right away." Frances [Kroll Ring, Fitzgerald's assistant] and I would look for a suitable ground-floor apartment nearby. Until then, he would stay with me.

Scott was a difficult patient. He made me promise I would not talk to the doctor alone. "I don't want him telling you anything he wouldn't tell me," he explained. On Dr. Wilson's visits, I was not to take him aside. I never questioned Dr. Wilson about the condition of Scott's heart.

I had tickets to a press preview of *This Thing Called Love*, a comedy starring Rosalind Russell and Melvyn Douglas. I hadn't gone to a preview in weeks. A comedy would be just the thing.

Scott dressed. He stood before the mirror fixing his bow tie. He gave it a final tug at both ends and threw a puckish glance at me. I was waiting at the door. "I always wanted to be a dandy," he said, with a grin. That night, Friday night, December 20, we went to the Pantages Theatre and saw *This Thing Called Love*.

When the film was over and the house lights came on, Scott stood up to let me by him into the aisle. I looked back just in time to see him stagger, as if someone had struck him off balance. He had to lean down and grab the arm rest for support. I thought he had stumbled. I hurried back and took his arm. He said, in a low, strained voice, "I feel awful—everything started to go as it did in Schwab's." I held his arm tightly. He said, "I suppose people will think I'm drunk." I said, "Scott, nobody saw it." I held him under his arm, supporting as much of his weight as I could without drawing attention, and we moved slowly up the aisle. A chill went through me as I realized that he had not pushed my hand away as he had done each time I had tried to help him in the past. I tried to appear in animated conversation with him as we made our way. I thought, furiously, he hasn't taken a drink in a year and now they'll all think he's drunk again.

We walked slowly to the car. The air revived him and he breathed deeply. "How do I look?" he asked. In the powerful lights of the Pantages, I could see him clearly. I said, "You look very pale. Shouldn't we call the doctor?"

Scott said no. Dr. Wilson was coming tomorrow, anyway. Let's not make any fuss.

He drove home slowly and by the time we had arrived, he felt better. He took his sleeping pills, went immediately to bed, and fell asleep.

I went into his room, later, and looked at him. He slept very peacefully, like a tired child.

I did not know that he would die the next day.

A bright noon-day sun shone through the window of my sitting room. I sat at the typewriter. Scott, comfortable in slacks, slippers, and a sweater over his shirt, paced up and down, dictating. It was a letter to Scottie from me, informing her that for Christmas I was sending her my fox-fur jacket and an evening dress. I knew Scottie, now in her junior year, could make good use of them. I felt a pang at giving up my jacket—but I wanted to please her.

Scott had awakened only a little before, having slept well. I brought him coffee as he sat up in bed, making notes for a new chapter. Then, restless, he had gotten up and dressed. Dr. Wilson was to come after lunch.

Frances dropped in, bringing Scott's mail, which still went to his apartment. There were a few bills, several advertisements, and the current issue of *The Princeton Alumni Weekly*. I gave Frances my dress and jacket which she promised to pack and mail. She left.

It was a little after two o'clock.

I prepared sandwiches and coffee for lunch while Scott glanced through the newspapers. I heard an exclamation. He began to read aloud: Germany, Italy, and Japan had signed a mutual-aid pact. He shook his head as he read. Though he was contemptuous of Mussolini, he respected Japan as a fighting power. This would force the United States into the war. Sooner or later we would be in it. If his book was a success, he went on, he would like to go to Europe and write about the war. And with a rueful smile, "Ernest won't have that field all to himself, then." Hemingway had written brilliantly about the Spanish Civil War: now he was sending special dispatches from Europe. And after the war, Scott was saying—if *The Last Tycoon* was a hit—I would give up my job, we would both live in the East and travel a great deal. He would care for me. Once before he had said, "If ever I get out of this mess, I'll make it up to you, Sheilo—"

After lunch he was restless. He went into the kitchen and I heard him moving around, opening cupboards. Then he reappeared. "I'm going to Schwab's to get some ice cream," he said.

"But you might miss the doctor—if it's something sweet you want, I've got some Hershey bars."

"Good enough," he said. "They'll be fine."

I brought him two chocolate bars from the box I kept by my bedside table. He picked up *The Princeton Alumni Weekly*, sank into his green armchair next to the fireplace, and began reading. As he read, he munched on the chocolate. I picked up one of my music books, curled up on the settee, and began reading about Beethoven.

Every little while we looked up and exchanged smiles. I noticed that Scott, with one of his stubby pencils, was making notes on the margin of an article about the Princeton football team. Again our eyes met: he grinned as he deliberately licked the chocolate from his fingers and bent down to his magazine again. I turned back to my book.

I saw, out of the corner of my eye—as you see something when you are not looking directly at it—I saw him suddenly start up out of his chair, clutch the mantelpiece and, without a sound, fall to the floor. He lay flat on his back, his eyes closed, breathing heavily.

When he stood up so unexpectedly I thought, *oh, he's stretching*. When he fell I thought, *oh, he's stumbled*. And then: *he's fainted!*

In the split second of that realization, as I sat there, willing myself to rise, yet not able, there was a choking, gasping sound in his throat.

Then I was up, and kneeling on the floor beside him, saying, "Scott—Scott—"

My mind whirled with thoughts. He's fainted. What do you do when someone faints? You pour brandy down his throat. But Scott's not been drinking—won't the taste of brandy start him off again? In the movies they loosen the collar—yes, that's sensible.

That's harmless. I loosened his collar.

I was on my knees, looking at him.

I thought, *this faint has lasted a long time.*

His body seemed to heave gently. I ought to do something. I'll call Dr. Wilson. No, he'll be here any minute. No, I must call him, I can't wait. What doctor *will* I call? No, the brandy. It must be brandy, right away.

I clambered to my feet and rushed into the dinette and found the brandy bottle and poured some into a glass and rushed back and poured some into his mouth. His teeth were clenched. I poured the brandy between his clenched teeth. I felt embarrassed. This was sacrilege—it was taking advantage of Scott. He wasn't there to wipe it off. I wiped it off with my hand.

I found myself at the telephone, calling Dr. Wilson. There was no answer. I ran my finger down the list of doctors and called one. "Someone's very ill—he's unconscious—can you come right over?"

Then I rushed out of the apartment and pounded on the door of Harry Culver, the manager of the building. "Come quickly—Mr. Fitzgerald has fainted and it's lasted so long. I'm getting frightened."

Mr. Culver was at my heels as I ran back. He knelt beside Scott and felt for his pulse. He looked up at me. "I'm afraid he's dead."

I thought, oxygen. I was at the telephone calling the fire department. Then the police. The door opened and Pat Duff, my secretary, entered. Then everything became confused. It seemed that I was still at the telephone when the apartment was full of people and soft voices and firemen with a Pulmotor were working over Scott and I heard myself saying again and again, "Hurry up, please, hurry up, please save him." Unexpectedly Buff Cobb was holding me close to her, the firemen were gone, and a white sheet covered Scott's body. I became hysterical. "Take that away, he won't be able to breathe, he'll suffocate, please, please!" Buff was leading me into another room. "You'll stay with us tonight," she was saying gently. "We'll take care of everything—" I broke away to rush into the sitting room and Scott's body was not there.

I began to cry. I cried but no sound came. The tears rolled down my cheeks but I made no sound.

A NOTE ON FITZGERALD

BY JOHN DOS PASSOS

THE NOTICES IN THE press referring to Scott Fitzgerald's untimely death produced in the reader the same strange feeling that you have when, after talking about some topic for an hour with a man, it suddenly comes over you that neither you nor he has understood a word of what the other was saying. The gentlemen who wrote these pieces obviously knew something about writing the English language, and it should follow that they knew how to read it. But shouldn't the fact that they had set themselves up to make their livings as critics of the work of other men furnish some assurance that they recognized the existence of certain standards in the art of writing? If there are no permanent standards, there is no criticism possible.

It seems hardly necessary to point out that a well written book is a well written book whether it's written under Louis XIII or Joe Stalin or on the wall of a tomb of an Egyptian Pharaoh. It's the quality of detaching itself from its period while embodying its period that marks a piece of work as good. I would have no quarrel with any critic who examined Scott Fitzgerald's work and declared that in his opinion it did not detach itself from its period. My answer would be that my opinion was different. The strange thing

73

about the articles that came out about Fitzgerald's death was that the writers seemed to feel that they didn't need to read his books; all they needed for a license to shovel them into the ashcan was to label them as having been written in such and such a period now past. This leads us to the inescapable conclusion that these gentlemen had no other standards than the styles of window-dressing on Fifth Avenue. It means that when they wrote about literature all they were thinking of was the present rating of a book on the exchange, a matter which has almost nothing to do with its eventual value. For a man who was making his living as a critic to write about Scott Fitzgerald without mentioning *The Great Gatsby* just meant that he didn't know his business. To write about the life of a man as important to American letters as the author of *The Great Gatsby* in terms of last summer's styles in ladies' hats, showed an incomprehension of what it was all about, that, to anyone who cared for the art of writing, was absolutely appalling. Fortunately there was enough of his last novel already written to still these silly yappings. The celebrity was dead. The novelist remained.

It is tragic that Scott Fitzgerald did not live to finish *The Last Tycoon*. Even as it stands I have an idea that it will turn out to be one of those literary fragments that from time to time appear in the stream of a culture and profoundly influence the course of future events. His unique achievement, in these beginnings of a great novel, is that here for the first time he has managed to establish that unshakable moral attitude towards the world we live in and towards its temporary standards that is the basic essential of any powerful work of the imagination. A firmly anchored ethical standard is something that American writing has been struggling towards for half a century.

During most of our history our writers have been distracted by various forms of the double standard of morals. Most of our great writers of the early nineteenth century were caught on the tarbaby of the decency complex of the period, so much more painful in provincial America than on Queen Grundy's own isle. Since the successful revolt of the realists under Dreiser, the dilemma has been different, but just as acute. A young American proposing to write a book is faced by the world, the flesh and the devil on the one hand and on the other by the cramped schoolroom of the highbrows with its flyblown busts of the European great and its priggish sectarian attitudes. There's popular fiction and fortune's bright roulette wheel, and there are the erratic aspirations of the longhaired men and shorthaired women who, according to the folklore of the time, live on isms and Russian tea, and absinthe and small magazines of verse. Everybody who has put pen to paper during the last twenty years has been daily plagued by the difficulty of deciding whether he's to do "good" writing that will satisfy his conscience or "cheap" writing that will satisfy his pocketbook. Since the standards of value have never been strongly established, it's often been hard to tell which was which. As a result all but the most fervid disciples of the cloistered muse have tended to try to ride both horses at once, or at least alternately. That effort and the subsequent failure to make good either aim, has produced hideous paroxysms of moral and intellectual obfuscation. A great deal of Fitzgerald's own life was made a hell by this sort of schizophrenia, that ends in paralysis of the will and of all the functions of body and mind. No durable piece of work, either addressed to the pulps or to the ages, has ever been accomplished by a doubleminded man. To attain the invention of any sound thing, no matter how trivial, demands the integrated effort of somebody's whole heart and whole intelligence. The agonized efforts of split personalities to assert themselves in writing has resulted, on the money side, in a limp pandering to every conceivable low popular taste and prejudice, and, on the angels' side, in a sterile connoisseur viewpoint that has made "good" writing, like vintage wines and old colonial chairs, a co-efficient of the leisure of the literate rich.

One reason for the persistence of this strange dualism and the resulting inefficiency of the men and women who have tried to create literature in this country is that few of us have really faced the problem of who was going to read what we wrote. Most of us started out with a dim notion of a parliament of our peers and our betters through the ages that would eventually screen out the vital grain. To this the Marxists added the heady picture of the onmarching avenging armies of the proletariat who would read your books round their campfires. But as the years ground on both the aristocratic republic of letters of the eighteenth century and the dreams of a universal first of May have receded further and further from the realities we have had to live among. Only the simple requirements of the editors of mass circulation magazines with income based on advertising have remained fairly stable, as have the demands of the public brothels of Hollywood, where retired writers, after relieving their consciences by a few sanctimonious remarks expressing what is known in those haunts as "integrity," have earned huge incomes by setting their wits to work to play up to whatever tastes of the average man seemed easiest to cash in on at any given moment.

This state of things is based, not, as they try to make us believe, on the natural depravity of men with brains, but on the fact that for peace as well as for war industrial techniques have turned the old world upside down. Writers are up today against a new problem of illiteracy. Fifty years ago you either learned to read and write or you didn't learn. The constant reading of the Bible in hundreds of thousands of humble families kept a basic floor of literacy under literature as a whole, and under the English language. The variety of styles of writing so admirably represented, the relative complexity of many of the ideas involved and the range of ethical levels to be found in that great compendium of ancient Hebrew culture demanded, in its reading and in its exposition to the children, a certain mental activity, and provided for the poorer classes the same sort of cultural groundwork that the study of Greek and Latin provided for the sons of the rich. A mind accustomed to the Old and New Testaments could easily admit Shakespeare and the entire range of Victorian writing: poetry, novels, historic and scientific essays, up to the saturation point of that particular intelligence. Today the English-speaking peoples have no such common basic classical education. The bottom level is the visual and aural culture of the movies, not a literary level at all. Above that appear all sorts of gradation of illiteracy, from those who, though they may have learned to read in school, are now bare-ly able to spell out the captions in the pictures, to those who can take in, with the help of the photographs, a few simple sentences out of the daily tabloids, right through to the several millions of actively lit-erate people who can read right through *The Saturday Evening Post* or *Reader's Digest* and understand every word of it. This is the literal truth. Every statistical survey that has recently been made of literacy in this country has produced the most staggering results. We have to face the fact that the number of Americans capable of reading a page of anything not aimed at the mentality of a child of twelve is not only on the decrease but probably rapidly on the decrease. A confused intimation of this situation has, it seems to me, done a great deal to take the ground from under the feet of intelligent men who in the enthusiasm of youth decided to set themselves up to be writers. The old standards just don't ring true to the quicker minds of this unstable century. Literature, who for? they ask themselves. It is natural that they should turn to the easy demands of the pop-ular market, and to that fame which if it is admittedly not death-less is at least ladled out publicly and with a trowel.

Scott Fitzgerald was one of the inventors of that kind of fame. As a man he was tragically destroyed by his own invention. As a writer his triumph was that he managed in *The Great Gatsby* and to a greater degree in *The Last Tycoon* to weld together again the two divergent halves, to fuse the conscientious worker that no cre-ative man can ever really kill with the moneyed celebrity who aimed his stories at the twelve-year-olds. In *The Last Tycoon* he was even able to invest with some human dignity the pimp and pander aspects of Hollywood. There he was writing, not for highbrows or for lowbrows, but for whoever had enough elementary knowledge of the English language to read through a page of a novel.

Stahr, the prime mover of a Hollywood picture studio who is the central figure, is described with a combination of intimacy and detachment that constitutes a real advance over the treatment of such characters in all the stories that have followed Dreiser and Frank Norris. There is no trace of envy or adulation in the picture. Fitzgerald writes about Stahr, not as a poor man writing about someone rich and powerful, nor as the impotent last upthrust of some established American stock sneering at a parvenu Jew; but coolly, as a man writing about an equal he knows and understands. Immediately a frame of reference is established that takes into the warm reasonable light of all-around comprehension the Hollywood magnate and the workers on the lot and the people in the dusty sunscorched bungalows of Los Angeles. In that frame of reference acts and gestures can be described on a broad and to a certain degree passionlessly impersonal terrain of common humanity.

This establishment of a frame of reference for common humanity has been the main achievement and the main utility of writing which in other times and places has come to be called great. It requires, as well as the necessary skill with the tools of the trade, secure standards of judgment that can only be called ethical. Hollywood, the subject of *The Last Tycoon*, is probably the most important and the most difficult subject for our time to deal with. Whether we like it or not it is in that great bargain sale of five and ten cent lusts and dreams that the new bottom level of our culture is being created. The fact that at the end of a life of brilliant worldly successes and crushing disasters Scott Fitzgerald was engaged so ably in a work of such importance proves him to have been the first-rate novelist his friends believed him to be. In *The Last Tycoon* he was managing to invent a set of people seen really in the round instead of lit by an envious spotlight from above or below. *The Great Gatsby* remains a perfect example of this sort of treatment at an earlier, more anecdotic, more bas relief stage, but in the fragments of *The Last Tycoon*, you can see the beginning of a real grand style. Even in their unfinished state these fragments, I believe, are of sufficient dimensions to raise the level of American fiction to follow in some such way as Marlowe's blank verse line raised the whole level of Elizabethan verse.

—1945

SCOTT FITZGERALD, AUTHOR DIES AT 44

WRITER OF *THE GREAT GATSBY* AND *THIS SIDE OF PARADISE* INTERPRETED "JAZZ ERA"

STRICKEN IN HOLLYWOOD

BRILLIANT NOVELIST OF TWENTIES, INACTIVE RECENTLY, LIKENED SELF TO "CRACKED PLATE"

HOLLYWOOD, CALIF., December 22, 1940 (AP)—F. Scott Fitzgerald, novelist, short story writer and scenarist, died at his Hollywood home yesterday. His age was forty-four. He suffered a heart attack three weeks ago.

Mr. Fitzgerald in his life and writings epitomized "all the sad young men" of the post-war generation. With the skill of a reporter and ability of an artist he captured the essence of a period when flappers and gin and "the beautiful and the damned" were the symbols of the carefree madness of an age.

Roughly, his own career began and ended with the Nineteen Twenties. *This Side of Paradise*, his first book, was published in the first year of that decade of skyscrapers and short skirts. Only six others came between it and his last, which, not without irony, he called *Taps at Reveille*. That was published in 1935. Since then a few short stories, the script of a moving picture or two, were all that came from his typewriter. The promise of his brilliant career was never fulfilled.

The best of his books, the critics said, was *The Great Gatsby*. When it was published in 1925 this ironic tale of life on Long Island at a time when gin was the national drink and sex the national obsession (according to the exponents of Mr. Fitzgerald's school of writers), it received critical acclaim. In it Mr. Fitzgerald was at his best, which was, according to John Chamberlain, his "ability to catch . . . the flavor of a period, the fragrance of a night, a snatch of old song, in a phrase."

This same ability was shown in his first book and its hero, Amory Blaine, became as much a symbol of Mr. Fitzgerald's own generation as, two years later, Sinclair Lewis's *Babbitt* was to become a symbol of another facet of American culture. All his other books and many of his short stories (notably "The Beautiful and Damned") had this same quality.

Francis Scott Key Fitzgerald (he was named after the author of the National Anthem, a distant relative of his mother's) was a stocky, good-looking young man with blond hair and blue eyes who might have stepped from the gay pages of one of his own novels. He was born September 24, 1896, at St. Paul, Minnesota, the son of Edward and Mary McQuillan Fitzgerald.

At the Newman School, in Lakewood, New Jersey, where he was sent, young Fitzgerald paid more attention to extracurricular activities than to his studies. When he entered Princeton in 1913 he had already decided upon a career as writer of musical comedies. He spent most of his first year writing an operetta for the Triangle Club and consequently "flunked" in several subjects. He had to spend the summer studying. In his sophomore year he was a "chorus girl" in his own show.

War came along in 1917 and Fitzgerald quit Princeton to join the Army. He served as a second lieutenant and then as a first lieutenant in the Forty-fifth and Sixty-seventh Infantry Regiments and then as aide de camp to Brig. Gen. J. A. Ryan.

Every Saturday he would hurry over to the Officers' Club and there "in a room full of smoke, conversation and rattling newspapers" he wrote a 120,000-word novel on the consecutive weekends of three months. He called it *The Romantic Egoist*. The publisher to whom he submitted it said it was the most original manuscript he had seen for years—but he wouldn't publish it.

After the war he begged the seven city editors of the seven newspapers in New York to give him a job. Each turned him down. He went to work for the Barron Collier advertising agency, where he penned the slogan for a Muscatine, Iowa, laundry: "We keep you clean in Muscatine."

This got him a raise, but his heart was not in writing cards for street cars. He spent all his spare time writing satires, only one of which he sold—for $30. He then abandoned New York in disgust and went back to St. Paul, where he wrote *This Side of Paradise*. Its flash and tempo and its characters, who, in the estimation of Gertrude Stein, created for the general public "the new generation," made it an immediate success.

At the same time he married Miss Zelda Sayre of Montgomery, Alabama, who has been called more than once "the brilliant counterpart of the heroines of his novels." Their only child, Frances Scott Fitzgerald, was born in 1921.

His next two books were collections of short stories: *Flappers and Philosophers* (1920) and *Tales of the Jazz Age* (1922). In 1923 he published a satirical play, *The Vegetable: or, From President to Postman*, and then for the next two years he worked on *The Great Gatsby*. He had gathered material for it while living on Long Island after the war, and all its characters were taken compositely from life. He wrote most of it in Rome or on the Riviera, where he also wrote his most successful short stories. These, in 1926, were gathered under the title *All the Sad Young Men*.

Only two other books were to follow: *Tender Is the Night* (1934) and *Taps at Reveille* (1935). After that, for several years, he lived near Baltimore, Maryland, where he suffered a depression of spirit which kept him from writing. He made several efforts to write but failed, and in an autobiographical article in *Esquire* likened himself to a "cracked plate."

"Sometimes, though," he wrote, "the cracked plate has to be retained in the pantry, has to be kept in service as a household necessity. It can never be warmed on the stove nor shuffled with the other plates in the dishpan; it will not be brought out for company but it will do to hold crackers late at night or to go into the ice-box with the left overs."

—*The New York Times*
December 23, 1940

NINE WOMEN PATIENTS DIE
IN HOSPITAL FIRE

WIDOW OF F. SCOTT FITZGERALD
ONE OF VICTIMS IN MENTAL
INSTITUTION IN ASHEVILLE

ASHEVILLE, N.C., March 11, 1948 (AP)—Fire swept through a mental hospital here early today and caused the death of nine women patients. Twenty others were led to safety.

Flames quickly engulfed the four-story central building of the Highland Hospital for Nervous Diseases. The cries of some of the twenty-nine women echoed over the grounds. Firemen, police, nurses, doctors and townspeople rushed to the rescue.

Seven women were trapped on the upper floors. Two others removed by firemen died in a short while. It was the third fire in the hospital in less than a year.

Fire Chief J. C. Fitzgerald said he believed today's fire started in the kitchen of the hospital's central building, but that had not been officially determined.

Dr. B. T. Bennett, hospital medical director, estimated the fire loss at $300,000.

Miss Betty Ubbenga of Lincoln, Illinois, assistant supervisor, described how she and Supervisor Frances Bender of Scarboro, West Virginia, first went after the helpless patients.

"We felt that the others were awake and would help themselves," she said. "As soon as we got the helpless ones out and safely put away elsewhere, we rushed back to help the others. By then we knew some had been trapped. Some of them were awake, we know, and were rousing the others."

Some of the patients had been overcome by smoke and were unable to help themselves, Miss Ubbenga said.

"It seemed no time at all until the entire building was like a furnace."

WIDOW OF AUTHOR A VICTIM

Mrs. F. Scott Fitzgerald, widow of the author and a victim of the hospital fire, had been ill for some years and went to the Highland Hospital three months ago from the home of her eighty-five-year-old mother, Mrs. Anthony Sayre in Montgomery, Alabama. Mrs. Fitzgerald's daughter, Mrs. S. J. Lanahan of this city, said burial would be in Rockville, Maryland, where the author is buried.

Mrs. Fitzgerald, who was forty-seven years old, was the author of a novel, *Save Me the Waltz*, and many short stories published in leading magazines. The Fitzgeralds were married in 1920. Mrs. Fitzgerald's father was Judge Anthony Sayre of the Alabama Supreme Court. Besides her mother and daughter, she leaves three sisters.

—*The New York Times*
March 12, 1948

FRANCES SCOTT SMITH
WRITER AND CHILD OF
THE FITZGERALDS

BY HERBERT MITGANG

F RANCES SCOTT SMITH, the only child of Zelda and F. Scott Fitzgerald, died of cancer yesterday at her home in Montgomery, Alabama. She was sixty-four years old.

Mrs. Smith, known as Scottie, lived partly in the shadow of her father, the author of *The Great Gatsby* and other novels, and her almost equally legendary mother, about whom two plays and the biography *Zelda* were written and who herself wrote the novel *Save Me the Waltz*.

But the famous couple's daughter carved out a life of her own, in part a literary one, writing for *The New Yorker* and contributing articles to *The Washington Post* and *The New York Times*, among other publications.

In the 1920s and 1930s, Scottie Fitzgerald's parents symbolized the dashing style of the Jazz Age. She once said that the Fitzgerald name opened doors for her but also had its drawbacks.

"I've always jokingly said that it was the best paid part-time job in the world," Mrs. Smith said in a recent interview. "It has been hard work sometimes, because it encompassed the whole period when my father got extremely popular."

Of her parents, she said, "They were always very circumspect around me. I was unaware of all the drinking that was going on. I was very well taken care of and I was never neglected. I didn't consider it a difficult childhood at all. In fact, it was a wonderful childhood."

Scottie Fitzgerald was born in 1921 in St. Paul, Minnesota, her father's hometown, and traveled and lived with them in France and in New York—including in Great Neck, the "West Egg" on Long Island that was the little-disguised fictional locale of *The Great Gatsby*. It was also the background for an article that her father wrote in the mid-1920s called, "How to Go Broke on $28,000 a Year," that defined the family's way of life.

The daughter entered Vassar College in 1938. In her college years, when her father was working in Hollywood, he wrote her letters of advice, later collected as *Letters to His Daughter*. She resided for a period with her father's literary agent, Harold Ober, in Scarsdale, New York. In her junior and senior years, she wrote and produced two campus musical comedies.

After graduating, she worked successively for *The New Yorker*, as a publicist for Radio City Music Hall, and as a researcher for Time-Life magazines. During World War II, she contributed to the Talk of the Town section of *The New Yorker*, wrote nightclub reviews, and also published her first piece of fiction there, called "The Stocking Present." She also wrote for a number of other magazines.

In 1953, she joined the staff of *The Democratic Digest*, published by the Democratic National Committee. She was an active volunteer and writer for Governor Adlai E. Stevenson, when he ran against President Eisenhower in 1956. That year she became a political columnist for *The Northern Virginia Sun*. She also wrote and directed musicals for the benefit of the Multiple Sclerosis Society of Washington.

Scottie Fitzgerald was married twice, to Samuel J. Lanahan in 1943 and to Clinton G. Smith in 1967. Both marriages ended in divorce.

She is survived by two daughters, Eleanor Lanahan Hazard of

Montgomery and Cecilia Scott Ross of Avondale, Pennsylvania, and a son, Samuel Jackson Lanahan of Eugene, Oregon.

Services are scheduled for Saturday at St. Mary's Church in Rockville, Maryland, with burial next to Zelda and F. Scott Fitzgerald in the church cemetery.

—*The New York Times*
June 19, 1986

TO CORRECT AN
ERRONEOUS IMPRESSION

A PRESS RELEASE FROM
CHARLES SCRIBNER'S SONS, F. SCOTT
FITZGERALD'S PUBLISHER

F. SCOTT FITZGERALD did not die "completely out of print." At his death in December of 1940, only *The Beautiful and Damned* had passed out of print, as of the previous September. *This Side of Paradise* and *The Vegetable* were available until July, 1941. *Tender Is the Night* and *Flappers and Philosophers* went out of print in July, 1942. The last sales of *Taps at Reveille*, *Tales of the Jazz Age* and *All the Sad Young Men* have the date of 1945, though apparently a few copies of each book were available until 1947. *The Great Gatsby* was never out of print. The last sale of the original trade edition is recorded in the year 1945. In 1941, however, *The Last Tycoon* was issued in a volume containing also *The Great Gatsby*, and five of the best known stories. That volume has been available ever since.

The widely quoted letter of F. Scott Fitzgerald to Maxwell Perkins, "I wish I was in print . . ." dated May 20, 1940, when read in its entirety is a wish to be in print in a diversity of ways—in the lower priced reprints, and so forth—as a means of averting the time when all his books would be unavailable through the disappearance of their original editions. Though that time was then clearly foreshadowed, it never became fact.

In 1951, all the novels of F. Scott Fitzgerald are in print, either in hardcover editions or in low-priced reprints. The project for a new collection of stories, the book issued in March of the present year, was set actively in motion more than two years ago, in January of 1949.

—April 25, 1951

ACKNOWLEDGMENTS

Essays of John Peale Bishop. Copyright 1948 by Charles Scribner's Sons. Reprinted by permission of the publisher and the estate of the author.

"Fitzgerald's First Flapper" by Amar Shah. Copyright © 2000 by Amar Shah. Reprinted by permission of the author.

"Scott Fitzgerald" from *A Moveable Feast* by Ernest Hemingway. Excerpted with permission of Scribner, a Division of Simon & Schuster. Copyright © 1964 by Mary Hemingway. Copyright renewed © 1992 by John H. Hemingway, Patrick Hemingway, and Gregory Hemingway.

"F. Scott Fitzgerald: The Man and His Work" by Alfred Kazin. Copyright 1951 by Alfred Kazin. Reprinted by permission of the estate of the author.

"Fitzgerald in Hollywood" by Budd Schulberg. Copyright 1941 by Editorial Publications, Inc. Reprinted by permission of the author.

Excerpt from *The Disenchanted* by Budd Schulberg. Copyright 1950 by Budd Schulberg. Reprinted by permission of the author.

"My Boss, F. Scott Fitzgerald" by Frances Kroll Ring. Copyright © 1964 by Frances Kroll Ring. Originally appeared in *Los Angeles*, January 1964. Reprinted by permission of the author.

Excerpt from "Footnotes on Fitzgerald" by Frances Kroll Ring. Copyright 1959 by Frances Kroll Ring. Originally appeared in *Esquire*, December 1959. Reprinted by permission of the author.

Excerpts from *Beloved Infidel* by Sheilah Graham. Copyright 1958 by Sheilah Graham and Gerold Frank. Reprinted by permission of Henry Holt and Company, Inc.

"A Note on Fitzgerald" by John Dos Passos. Originally appeared in *The Crack-up* edited by Edmund Wilson. A shorter version of this essay appeared in *The New Republic*, February 17, 1941. Reprinted by permission of the Estate of John Dos Passos.

"Scott Fitzgerald, Author, Dies at 44" originally appeared in *The New York Times*, December 28, 1940. Copyright 1940 by *The New York Times*. Reprinted by permission.